CRISIS
and
REPETITION

Essays on Art and Culture

Kate Armstrong

Michigan State University Press
East Lansing

∞ The paper used in this publication meets the minimum requirements
of ANSI/NISO Z39.48-1992 (R 1997) (Permanence of Paper).

Michigan State University Press
East Lansing, Michigan 48823-5202

Printed and bound in the United States of America.

08 07 06 05 04 03 02   1 2 3 4 5 6 7 8 9 10

Library of Congress Cataloging-in-Publication Data

Crisis & repetition : essays on art and culture / Kate Armstrong.
    p.   cm.
Includes bibliographical references.
    ISBN 0-87013-596-1 (pbk. : alk. paper)
    1. Aesthetics, Modern.   2. Repetition (Aesthetics)   3. Death of God
theology.   I. Title: Crisis and repetition.   II. Title.
    BH301.R46 A76 2001
    111'.85—dc21   2001005746

Cover design by Heather Truelove
Book design by Jim Buchanan of Bookcomp, Inc.

Visit Michigan State University Press on the World Wide Web at:
www.msupress.msu.edu

CRISIS
and
REPETITION

To Michael Tippett

ACKNOWLEDGMENTS

*With myriad thanks to
J. A. Bradley and
the Jockey Club*

Contents

Figures

CRISIS
and
REPETITION

Introduction

UNDERLYING THE ISSUES that come to light in the course of these essays is the notion of crisis emerging from the continental philosophical and theological tradition. Crisis is connected to the disappearance of the transcendent realm, the disappearance of absolutes, of authoritative standards that reason can access; in short, the disappearance of God and the Word of God. Without God, the "guarantor of meaning," the human realm becomes untethered from the transcendent and is left with the radical historicism that results when there is nothing beyond the realm of historical time. "Death of God" theologians, such as Thomas J. J. Altizer, begin with the notion that a different sense of immanence—and therefore history—emerges from the crisis of the disappearance of the transcendent. For Altizer, historicism is the result of this crisis because the insertion of the transcendent into the immanent realm is a necessary condition of history. But at this point some background on the tradition of death of God theology is needed in order to clarify what is at issue when addressing the displacement of the transcendent realm into the immanent.

I begin with Søren Kierkegaard's notion of the Incarnation as a model for the "coming-into-being" of all things. Although Kierkegaard does not do away with the transcendent realm due to his conviction that God is central to human life, it is his view that the movement from potentiality to actuality operates in the model of God becoming flesh in Jesus. For Kierkegaard, history is ruptured at the instant of the Incarnation, an idea that has application to Altizer's radical immanence. Altizer views Kierkegaard as the first modern theologian because Kierkegaard's leap of faith comes with this rupture, and because repetition comes into play as a way of propelling history forward within the realm of the immanent.

Kierkegaard formulates his concept of repetition in history using the Hegelian categories of objectivity and subjectivity in response to the

1

advent of a reality that is separate from faith. In *The Sickness unto Death*, Kierkegaard understands the central feature of Christianity, belief, to be antithetically related to the *cogito*, in which thought is the principal mode of apprehension. Objective knowledge, in his estimation, is not neutral but antithetical to the subjectivity of faith. God is banished from the "real" world when objectivity buys the option on reality. For Kierkegaard, it is not only God but also the individual who is banished from the "real," because faith, in his view, is crucial for the individual. He writes that the individual is "incommensurable from reality." Altizer describes the dilemma for Kierkegaard's individual in the following way: "So radical is this incommensurability that the existing individual and objective reality now exist in a state of dialectical opposition: to know objectively is to cease to exist subjectively, to exist subjectively is to cease to know objectively."[1]

Conceived of in this way, knowledge is profane because it is divorced from the transcendent realm of God. When faith is antithetically related to objectivity it becomes, according to Kierkegaard, absurd. Faith, then, is subjective because it exists through the negation of objectivity and is perpetuated by the repetition of this negation.

Like Kierkegaard, Altizer is adamant that the Incarnation not be treated as a one-time offer long since expired. Rather it represents an ongoing process of becoming. Before I address Altizer's notion of becoming, I will examine Nietzsche's thought on this topic in order to provide a comparison.

For Nietzsche the transcendent God supplants the selfhood of the individual. Nietzsche asks the individual to "kill" God, meaning that the individual must actively engage the radical immanence that results from God's "death." For Nietzsche, men achieve "godlike" stature by rising to the demands of the will; the self-empowered creature/creator wills his/her own actions in the midst of the chaos of radical immanence. The "death" of God redeems man by releasing him from the "other," which has hitherto been the locus of meaning, namely the unreachable, transcendent God to which man has had to appeal in the past.

In *Thus Spake Zarathustra*, Nietzsche images a new prophet who announces the end of Western history, which will be followed by an entirely new stage of historical development. When Zarathustra states that "God is dead," he posits the advent of a new era in which the transcendent God disappears, leaving behind the mere realm of human experience that is transformed at that instant into radical immanence. In the absence of a transcendent God, any supreme "vantage point" disappears and the world passes into meaninglessness and chaos because there is no longer any fixed ground or point of reference. For Nietzsche this immersion into chaos is a moment of crisis that introduces a new world in which previous forms and structures are reversed.

Nietzsche's concept of eternal recurrence starts out from infinite repetition as a gloomy picture of the chaos that results in a world without absolute meaning. Altizer writes that it is the "dialectical inversion of the Biblical category of the Kingdom of God."[2] When the role of the creator is displaced, the center is everywhere, manifest in all things in an eternally present moment. The transcendent becomes the immanent; the sacred becomes the profane. Potentiality becomes actualized, or actualizable in the "now." The world as a creation is displaced by the world as chaos; meaning and order are freed and an authentic nothingness presents itself to be embraced and willed toward art.

When fixed meanings and values are discarded, the chaos of the world recurs eternally. The individual's first reaction to this new world, the recognition of the totality of meaninglessness, is rejection, a radical "no-saying." Altizer writes that the shock and terror resulting from this chaotic state of crisis allows humanity to "peer into the abyss," which is the ground of all "no-saying" because "guilt and resentment are rooted in the interior reality of chaos and emptiness."[3]

But no-saying is quickly tempered by its dialectic opposite, "yes-saying." The new Zarathustra teaches yes-saying, which "embod[ies] a total affirmation of meaninglessness and horror."[4] Yes-saying reflects a final *cooincidentia oppositorum*, a merging of terror and joy, of history and eternity; profane emptiness and nothingness shift into a "sacred totality" that, by drawing everything into itself, negates its original form of no-saying, of terror at the void. Nietzsche asks the individual to will eternal recurrence, which means willing the eternal present that unfolds in every moment. When the individual wills the present it does not matter that the world is eternally repetitive; what matters is that every moment be treated by the individual as a moment in which to live fully and completely.[5] This is what Nietzsche means when he asks the individual to "kill" God.

Yes-saying and no-saying therefore operate in a dialectic. Once the fall of the transcendent realm has been ratified, the challenge facing humanity is the conceptualization of the new immanent landscape. Previously "tethered" meaning (or its impossibility) is released into the formless chaos of the immanent where Nietzsche's individual must forge a path through yes-saying and will.

Thus eternal recurrence refers ultimately to the most absolute affirmation of human activity. It proposes to reward the individuals who choose to accept the challenge of the "now," including that which is required in the way of will and strength. That individual is one who accepts the historical continuum, who is brave enough to exist in God's absence.

The death of God, therefore, removes transcendence from human consciousness and immerses the world into a state of absolute immanence. The individual is given the choice to embrace the godless world with complete joy—total affirmation of actual and immediate existence—or to retract in horror at the void. In this model, man is "liberated" from transcendent grounding: "Here the disappearence of transcendence actualizes a new immanence, as a total yes-saying to an immediate and actual present transforms transcendence into immanence, and absolute immanence dawns as the final kenotic metamorphosis of Spirit into flesh."[6]

For both Nietzsche and Altizer, the process of will is needed to characterize the immanent as a positive, creative force. Altizer is asking us to will the death and dissolution of all that has been in order to arrive at a new Christianity informed by radical immanence.

Nietzsche's statement "being begins in every now" characterizes the relationship between the sacred and the profane in a radically immanent world. What is crucial here is that all moments present themselves in the "now"; there is no other time or being to which deference is appropriate. Without the transcendent God, the immanent realm invites the individual to become a "creator," or a "god." The lack of a center means that every moment and every place is at the center when God as the "guarantor of meaning" is toppled from the central position. Radical immanence transforms the profane realm into the sacred realm without making it sacred: although it is transformed by the kenotic emptying of the sacred, the profane remains profane.

By "kenosis" Altizer means that God is present only in self-emptying or self-negation. The essence of kenosis, as will be further elucidated in the following chapters, is that God empties itself out through the process of changing forms. The transcendent God becomes kenotic though the Incarnation, through which God changes into the human form of Jesus, thus becoming "other" than itself. For Altizer, the new immanent God is not a transcendent creator but a God that *is* its creative acts of self-unfolding.

Altizer believes that this is what allows the Christian to embrace Jesus: the idea that the sacred "becomes" in every moment, and that therefore nostalgia for past forms of Christianity are meaningless, outmoded. He conceives of the Incarnation as "recurrent reality beginning anew in every Now."[7]

One difference between Nietzsche's and Altizer's notions of immanence is that Nietzsche celebrates immanence as a nonspiritual, or non-God, condition, whereas Altizer believes that kenosis brings God into the actualized realm, thereby ushering in a new era of Christianity that operates wholly within the immanent. Altizer believes that in order for Christianity to respond to Nietzche's call for the death of God in a manner of yes-saying, it cannot revert to previous transcendent conceptions of God. Altizer seeks to affirm immanence as a kenotic unfolding of God and to therefore revitalize the project of Christianity in the face of the "death" of the transcendent God.

The dialectic that emerges in Altizer's thought is that of Spirit into flesh: Spirit becomes its own "other" in the process of kenosis, whereas for Nietzsche, as we have seen, it is yes-saying and no-saying that play in an acceptance of the chaotic, newly godless world and that prosper from the drive of will. Altizer believes that God is not unchanging and unmoving but a perpetual "forward moving process of self negation, pure negativity, or kenotic metamorphosis."[8]

Whereas Nietzsche's concept of eternal recurrence is essentially anthropomorphic—it is solely a matter of the human realm—Altizer and Kierkegaard both deal with the metaphysical processes by which God becomes known and by which God becomes manifest in history, processes that are not exclusively human. An example of this that we have already considered is Kierkegaard's concept of the "coming-into-being" of all things as they emerge into the immanent from the transcendent.

I will now continue with a more specific analysis of these issues with relation to the following chapters. For my purposes, the crucial issue is the crisis that ensues with the transformation or displacement of the transcendent God, whether it be, as in Nietzsche's formulation, a complete disappearance that occasions humanity to confront chaos and transform it into the celebratory, creative yes-saying , or, as in Altizer's conception, where the death of God marks a new opportunity for Spirit to be understood in a radically immanent way through kenosis. It is this crisis, as played out within varied systems of thought and representation, that is explored in the chapters that follow.

The notion of crisis has two applications in my analysis. The first is an attempt to deal with notions of the "unrepresentable" in both writing and art, an exploration of what is left "beyond" representation when the transcendent is absent. This points us in the direction of Jacques Derrida's "impossible," Martin Heidegger's *das Ereignis*, the Marquis de Sade's outrage/transgression, Søren Kierkegaard's paradox, and to notions of the transcendental signified in the economy of representation that is constantly figured and refigured in the work of both the abstract expressionists and Andy Warhol. I have attempted to show how in the work of these thinkers and artists there is a common incommunicable, hidden element operating that is beyond intelligibility.

For Kierkegaard, there is still a transcendent God; for Altizer, there is still an immanent God; for other proponents of crisis, God has disappeared entirely. Yet there is a startling congruence in these different systems. One of the things I have tried to do is to explore "where" God goes when it disappears; or, to put it another way, what takes God's place when it disappears. It is my view that something ends up taking the place of God in each of these systems. This is not to say that what is replaced is analogous to God, but that there must be something in every system that cannot be fully understood or fully cognized: the unrepresentable.

This project, then, is first an attempt to frame these thinkers and artists in relation to so-called death of God theology so as to demonstrate that, by inverting or shifting the transcendent and the immanent, they are involved in a process of refiguring the divine. They are either relocating the divine in the immanent, elevating the immanent to the status of the divine, or working with this shift through paradox, thereby illustrating the impossibility of a totalizing system. Second, this project is an attempt to show that the ways they do this are related to writing or representing the unwritable or unrepresentable, and that the major strategy for this process is repetition.

THE UNREPRESENTABLE

I have set out to look at these thinkers in terms of what is being done with representation or its impossibility at various points, to locate in which of the systems the transcendental posit remains "out there" and in which of them it becomes an impossibility.

Implicit in my use of the term "representation" is the notion that traditionally, much pictorial portrayal is primarily an effort to re-present something that exists in the world. This is a notion that is transformed in postmodernism when the transcendent God is displaced because in God's absence there is no longer any "where" to "re-present" from. Works of art refer only to themselves. In a radically immanent world, a painting is an original referent that does not attempt to re-present something that already exists in the world, but only attempts to "present" itself.

Heidegger is central in some of these chapters because his notion of the Event leads to a new understanding of the unrepresentable. Heidegger's Event is an unfamiliar, unintelligible element that is the basis of his thinking. In "The Unrepresentable Event in Heidegger and Heizer," I have attempted to offer an analysis of the fluctuation between presence and absence in the representational economy of the sculptures of Michael Heizer with relation to Heidegger's notion of the Event in order to demonstrate that Heizer's refusal to "negate negation" is a subversion of representationality that parallels Heidegger's refusal to articulate the inarticulable Event.

In "Kierkegaard, History, and Modern Art," I've attempted to trace "nothingness" through the unrepresentable. I have looked at representations of nothingness in order to explore notions of an "origin" to which the conditions of existence refer. Heidegger discusses "Boundary" as that place from which things begin "presencing," and alternately, the Event as the principle through which "it" "gives."

My project in that chapter was to attempt to trace the figural representation of the "transcendental signified," the "now-vacant" site of God in crisis in the canvases of Barnett Newman, Kasimir Malevich, and Ad Reinhardt. I have applied the figural representations of this transcendent site to Kierkegaard's philosophy in order to suggest that Kierkegaard's theories of God, history, and repetition find significant applications to abstract expressionism.

As a way of relating repetition to notions of the unrepresentable, I would like to draw attention to Derrida's theory of the missing piece in language, the "impossible," which, if it were possible, would serve to connect the endless play of signification, ensuring intelligibility. Because this is impossible, the only option left is to gesture to the potential "site" of this "impossible" element, the empty site of the transcendent. This gesture is metaphorical, signaling not the actual "now-vacant" site of God, but a site "beyond" intelligibility that can only be gestured to and never explained.

It is difficult to characterize the unrepresentable without referring to explicit examples. Let it suffice to say at this point that each of the chapters works with this theme. For the time being I will explain this through the more tangible strategy of repetition in order to lay the foundations of more general statements about where the unrepresentable is and how it comes to be "figured."

REPETITION

Throughout this work I am also concerned with repetition as a strategy of figuring that which is unfigurable in the economy of language and representation. It is my view that repetition has great significance for an understanding of these thinkers.

In the context of crisis, repetition serves in two ways. The first is repetition as an ontological posit of the process of "coming-into-being" in history. I have chosen to look at this with reference to Kierkegaard, whose system is an example of a transcendent God that operates through the immanent realm, introducing the possibility that God, as transcendent, does not remain wholly "other" from the human realm. For Kierkegaard, the example of the Incarnation is a model of the way all things move from potentiality to actuality through God. This is significant in Kierkegaard because he maintains that the process of history is cyclical rather than linear, thus introducing repetition as a principle in its operation. By casting history in a nonlinear trajectory Kierkegaard means to emphasize the repetitive process of actualization as it is produced in the model of the Incarnation. Repetition figures into this process because the Incarnation, as conceived by Kierkegaard, functions within a series of figurations of Jesus within the historical continuum.

Jesus is prefigured, figured, and repeated through history, as are all other events that become actualized, that "come-into-being." This ontological repetition stands in contrast to a merely sequential view of history in which the unfolding of history is both a unidirectional and rational process.

The second way that repetition functions in this framework is within the works themselves, as is the case with Andy Warhol's repetition of the image. Warhol's image serves to illustrate how that which is represented can be repeated to the point where it can actually transcend its representation and gesture to the unrepresentable. The gesture to the unrepresentable that is articulated through this strategy of incessant repetition introduces notions of the absent transcendent, the impossible, unrepresentable "beyond" that is summoned through the deceptively "empty" postmodern image of Warhol. This, of course, places it in relation to death of God theology and introduces two possible roles of the transcendent in relation to the immanent, and the immanent in relation to the transcendent: whether the transcendent is "full," as for Kierkegaard, or "empty" as it might be assumed to be in the instance of the "death" of God.

Repetition as a Process of Historicism

The first way that repetition functions in the context of crisis in this collection is in the context of history itself. Repetition arises as a strategy of interpreting the process of history once history is untethered from linearity. For example, Kierkegaard offers repetition as an answer to how things "come-into-being" from the transcendent to the immanent. Now in Kierkegaard's case, there is not an explicit absence of God; on the contrary, for him God is the central force in human life. He explicitly embraces the presence of a transcendent realm in the form of the Christian creator-God. But his theory has new applications in the work of death of God theologians such as Altizer. Kierkegaard maintains that everything comes into being in the model of the Incarnation, that the manifestation of God in the human form of Jesus represents the movement from potentiality into actuality, from transcendence into immanence. For Kierkegaard, this "coming-into-being" is not linear but cyclical, as everything is prefigured in some form in the movement from potentiality into actuality.[9]

The connection between Kierkegaard's repetition and Altizer's theology lies in the radically immanent kenosis that Altizer posits in reaction to the crisis of the death of God. For Altizer, the unfolding of history is the self-emptying, self-unfolding process of God as it is manifest in the immanent realm. Altizer's thought has repercussions for a conception of repetition as a process of history, for the role of immanence in the absence of a transcendent God, and also for repetition as a strategy of transcending meaning. In "Warhol and Kenosis," Altizer's radical immanence is taken as the starting point in an examination of Warhol's repetition of the image. This brings me to the second application of repetition.

Transcendence through Repetition

The second strategy of repetition is the attempt to figure the unfigurable through a repetition of the signifier that, in excess, leads to a transcendence of the signifier. The resulting transcendence of meaning doubles for the lost transcendent realm that is the impetus for the repetition in the first place. When signification is cut loose from notions of transcendent meaning, the sign becomes the "sign of a sign." The sign operates within an endless play of meanings that cannot refer to any referent in the absence of the transcendent realm.

One of my approaches to this phenomenon has been to show how the incessant repetition of a sign actually results in a gesture to the transcendent realm, a gesture to that which cannot be figured within the painting or work. I have tried to explain this in "Repetition and Utopia in Warhol and the Marquis de Sade," which posits Warhol's repetition as an attempt to diffuse meaning to the point where it gestures away from the image given within the painting, toward that which is "beyond." In the context of crisis, the sign functions in Warhol and Sade as the sign of a sign rather than the sign of an object that is re-presented through art or writing. The emptiness of the sign of the sign refers also to notions of the limit of representability, because it is a feature of postmodernism that there is no longer anywhere to present from, no longer anything "out there" to re-present. There is only presentation, always at once original and copied because there is no longer a "true" original realm to which things might refer. Warhol uses signs of signs in succession to repeat into nothingness, to transcend what is represented. This he achieves through repetition.

As I have shown in "Warhol and Kenosis," the image empties itself out in a manner that is parallel to God's self-emptying process of kenosis. For Altizer, God is present in the immanent realm through this kenotic emptying. The radical immanence that is represented in Warhol's paintings through the repetition of the image is nevertheless a process that is unrepresentable. In addition to the fact that it is untotalizable and must remain placed within an infinite series, the gesture to what is "beyond" the image, the transcendent "absence" (or, as Altizer calls it, the "present absence") can only be marked by the gesture away from the image itself. Warhol's incessant image is one strategy for figuring what is unfigurable, the same project to which the abstract expressionists take the opposite approach by their focus on the portrayal of the "transcendental signified," the vast nonrepresentational void.

Another illustration of this repetitive capacity that attempts to figure the unfigurable is Kierkegaard's paradoxical, fragmentary process of writing, which he employs in order to point to that which cannot be made explicit in the text. His pseudonymous writing is an excellent example of one of the ways the authority of the author is questioned, as is his fragmentary style that refuses the propositional-conceptual function of traditional language in order to point beyond what is actually written. Kierkegaard figures man's attempt at unity with the divine by writing in the interstices of intelligibility; in effect, he writes the impossible and the unwritable through paradox. This is explored in connection to the representational "beyond" that is figured in abstract expressionism in the section, "Kierkegaard, History, and Modern Art."

An additional paradox at the heart of Kierkegaard's thought is the attempt of the individual to mediate himself through his relationship with the divine, which is totally "other" and yet more fundamental than the previous stages of development within the human realm, the aesthetic and the ethical. In this, the individual attempts the impossible, that is, to at once transcend himself and to "get to" himself through his relationship with the divine.

Like Kierkegaard's techniques for subverting meaning through repetition, the Marquis de Sade's strategies of writing are also twofold. As explored in "Repetition and Utopia in Warhol and the Marquis de Sade,"

Sade's system revolves around the transgressive outrage that is performed through apathetic repetition. Apathetic repetition drives the actor to commit the act over and over again, until it is meaningless. In one way, Sade inverts theology by placing the outrage on the transcendent site where God "used" to be, beyond the limit of intelligibility and accessibility. Repetition is the only way to perform the outrage, and even then it is merely symbolic, an attempt to ultimately transgress the immanent realm in which the act takes place. The outrage has "always already" taken place through repetition, and yet it has also never taken place at all because the outrage/transgression cannot be accomplished in itself. In addition to being "always already" repeated according to the principle of apathetic repetition, the act is recorded through Sade's writing, repeating it on another level. Sade attempts to convey transgression through the acts he portrays in writing, but it is doubly impossible because he has posited the outrage in the realm of the transcendent, a principle that is always "other," always inaccessible. This parallels the other attempts at figuring the unfigurable through repetition. There is at once the act and the writing of the act that "always already" repeats the act.

The Sadean outrage/transgression can also be cast in the framework of Altizer's radical immanence. Sade relocates the divine in the immanent and the sacred in the profane in a way that facilitates the Sadean outrage as a sacred act, an act that attempts to unify the profane and the sacred through repetition in the same way that Warhol's repetition of the image uses immanent, empty images to deflect off one another and onto a transcendent realm "behind" the image. Warhol conceives of this unification of the sacred and profane in multivalent ways: the unification of high art with low, the sacrosanct image of the movie star with the sacrifice of the electric chair, the collapse of the celebrity with the commodity, the original with the copy.

Warhol empties himself into machinelike existence. He empties the image into nothingness, transcending the meaning of the image that is represented, thereby transcending what is represented. The image is repeated into nothingness through the repetition of the image within the image. In this, the image can be seen to figure the transcendent through the radically immanent, as parallel to Altizer. The image can also be seen as a process of fetishization of the image/object, which parallels the Sadean approach with outrage/transgression. Either Warhol figures the divine in the event of the death of the divine, or Warhol inverts the site of the divine to radical immanence, so as to elevate the immanent to the divine.

Furthermore, the Sadean repetition of the outrage is parallel to Altizer's kenosis as developed in "Warhol and Kenosis." For Warhol it is meaning and significance that are erased through repetition. For Altizer it is God, the "guarantor of meaning," that empties itself into the immanent through the repetitive unfolding of kenosis. The realm that remains "outside" can be conceived of traditionally, as with the creator-God, as a plenitude, a fullness of meaning. It can also be seen to represent an emptiness or ambiguity of what remains unassailable, inaccessible. For Sade, the outrage is striking for being intensely random, a mere inversion of Christian doctrine. It is only the possibility of the ambiguous triumph of transgressing transgression itself that forms the basis of Sade's principles. Since meaning and significance are erased through the repetitions that are necessary to inspire the outrage, the outrage itself—as it is posited transcendently—is an absence. Like Warhol and Altizer, image or God or outrage mark the absence of the transcendent realm, which can only be a "present absence."

What follows is thus an attempt to place these thinkers and artists in relation to death of God theology in order to show that by inverting or shifting the transcendent and the immanent they are involved in a process of refiguring the divine. They relocate the divine to the immanent, whether in Kierkegaard's manner, which retains the transcendent, or in Altizer's method, which recasts God as a principle of self-negation, or they elevate the immanent to the status of the divine, necessitating a gesture away from the immanent to the incommunicable "otherness" of the realm outside the representational economy. The shift between immanent and transcendent can also be broached by stretching the parameters of the medium so as to illustrate its limits and afford a new subjectivity through the text. Kierkegaard's paradox, duration in Warhol's films, Heizer's nonrepresentational unrepresentable, and the transgressive outrage of apathetic reiteration in the writing of the Marquis de Sade are projects that articulate their own impossibility.

The death of God requires an adjustment in meaning, history, the sacred, the authority of text and author, and representation. Kierkegaard, Newman, Warhol, Heidegger, Heizer, and Sade can all be seen to be transgressing meaningful linguistic and representational systems in order to subvert their own texts. The fragments that rupture Kierke-gaard's writing carve out a new path along which the reader is led to an understanding of what cannot be written. The vast blackness of abstract canvases turn out to be sites from which God is absent; the disruptive stripes dividing Newman's paintings are arrows directed at the unfigur-able vanishing point. The Marilyn Monroes turn out to be portraits of God. The rerouted eroticism in Sade turns into a refiguration of the sacred that appears when God dies.

Themes of the unrepresentable and repetition are explored in rela-tion to notions of crisis in order to elucidate their application to the work of writers and artists who have no outward similarity. In post-modern crisis, textual transgression takes place through the rupture that conceals and withdraws when named. Like traditional notions of the name of God, which disappears when named, the postmodern "impos-sible" retracts and withdraws when it is described. In other words, it cannot be described, but only gestured to. Repetition displaces mono-lithic systems of representation; it displaces temporal order and the order of meaning. It inspires the transcendence of what is represented within an image or text and leads toward notions of erasure, ecstasy, subver-sion, transgression, and rupture. I have tried to discern the ways in which this happens.

Chapter One

Repetition and Utopia in Warhol and the Marquis de Sade

IN THIS CHAPTER I WILL COMPARE the work of the eighteenth-century writer the Marquis de Sade and the twentieth-century painter Andy Warhol in reference to what I will call apathetic reiteration and the functional distance emerging from repetition. The work of both Warhol and Sade revolves around the pursuit of apathy and the erasure of significance: it is my view that they explore the transcendence of an act or an object through distance. Repetition is held up as a method of suppressing the significant in order to proliferate an image or an act into meaninglessness.

This process of distancing results for Warhol in the creation of the artist as machine and relates repetition to the commodification of desire emerging from the principle of consumption. Warhol's distance is manifest in the removal of audience identification with the event on-screen and in the focus on the surface quality of the image that repeats it into insignificance. He thereby disallows an emotive response to his work and offers a sense of apathy that seduces the viewer with the same tension between identification and emptiness as is evident in Sade's characters.

For Sade, distance through repetition results in the pursuit of the habitual crime as it evolves into apathy and creates the monster. Sade's repetition aims to foster total apathy that will habitualize the criminal act. His desire is an "always already" unfulfilled force that impels his characters toward more acts of apathetic crime. The outrage is posited as an act that must be completed without regret or remorse. His characters are driven by the desire to remain unaffected by their crimes, taking pleasure in their ability to repress, and consequently eliminate, morality. The characters install as much distance between themselves and the completion of the act as possible, finding pleasure in the interstice where the self is suspended in place of the apathetic monster and is eventually replaced by it.

Sade's process of writing mirrors the philosophy of apathetic repetition in that it represents a deferred repetition in itself. By writing the act, Sade repeats it in order to record it as it is "always already" repeated in the pursuit of apathetic repetition. The process of writing depends on the creation and maintenance of distance. Repetition becomes a system of distancing and a transcendence of the space of the representable for the act, and for the portrayal of the act in the writing process. The works themselves are figured as much by apathetic reiteration as are the processes of recording them. These artists integrate the act they record into the process of recording it, thereby changing the relationship between writing and doing into one in which writing and doing are fused in a repetitive loop.

I will also discuss the role that transcendence plays in these works as they address the process of entering into the space beyond what is represented. This notion of transcendence is comparable in principle to Sade's crime, which is repeated over and over again in order to cauterize the sensibilities of the actor. The transcendence of morality takes the subject into a new realm that cannot be elucidated beyond an explanation of the repetitions required for this transcendence. It is the process of arriving at the unspeakable through a transcendence of the known by way of repetition.

This idea of transcendence is present in the concepts of Sade's habitual crime as well as in Sade's writing, both of which repeat what was "always already" repeated. In Warhol this repetition is evident in the duration that structures his cinema, transcending what is explicit and resulting in a new way of looking, and also in his filmic reflections of seemingly unmediated events that reconstitute the act by making it indistinguishable from its transcription. These authors arrive at a new sense of the interrelationship between the act and the recording of the act by offering simulacra in place of images of the represented act or object.

In the second part of this essay I will look at the worlds constructed through these works as indicating the creation and maintenance of sacred/profane spaces that parody the utopian concept. In his writing Sade presents a castle/dungeon/boudoir that parodies these spaces in the outside world, recreating them as parodies of the prison where torture and punishment are inverted to represent pleasure and desire, whereas Warhol articulates the death drive present in American culture, making the underside visible by celebrating the "stars of the out-take" in a perversion of Hollywood cinema. He parodies the Hollywood film factory by creating an alternative Factory that collapses narrative structure and resituates the process of recording within a mode of campy perversion that theatricalizes everyday life by presenting it without editing or mediation. It is my view that the processes of writing explored by Sade and Warhol are themselves integral to the creation of these spaces because these processes depend on the kind of repetition that the work explores.

METHOD

There are two ways that Warhol parallels this apathetic repetition. The first is through a mechanization of the artist that emphasises the seriality of the works produced and removes authorship from them. He does this through the commodification of the image and by presenting what appears to be an unmediated portrayal of his subjects. He wants to erase himself as a human agent and replace himself as a machine in order to arrive at a purely standardized portrayal, recording life without comment. By recording it machinelike, however, Warhol makes the only comments that are important here: life is consumption, surface is everything, and apathy through repetition is the goal to which he aspires in his standardized universe.

Warhol-as-machine functions to reduce everything, including himself, to surface. By taking on the function of the recording machines, such as the camera and the tape recorder, Warhol also implicitly projects himself into the other machines, the death machines, manifest in his electric chair silk-screens and car crashes.[1] He is as apathetic to these images as he is to his soup cans: he produces in order to witness, passively. Peter Wollen writes: "It is as if by submerging himself into machine-like-ness, Warhol could enter, in phantasy, a world . . . in which, at one and the same time, the "otherness" of the image of the other was effaced and the identity of the self obliterated through the agency of an impersonal machine-like Other. Thus imaginary difference [is] erased and the identity of the subject reduced to the purely symbolic dimension of the name, functioning like a logo."[2] This brings me to the second way Warhol's work handles the principle of apathetic repetition.

Warhol enlarges time in order to paralyze the sensibilities of the audience. This enlarged sense of time is especially evident in his early films such as *Sleep*,[3] which depicts six hours of a man sleeping. He inspires two contrary responses by refusing audience identification: both responses correspond with Sade's struggle to remain impassive, to emerge apathetic. By fixing the eye of his camera on a limited space inside of which limited action takes place for extended periods of time, Warhol forces a violent, perverse process of endurance on the spectator. There is something slightly masochistic about the experience of looking at this minimalized activity for the full duration because the ability to engage the action on-screen is refused at every turn. Conversely, there is something peaceful in the resulting emptiness. There is an impulse to simply watch and remain passive. But when the action refuses to unfold, when it remains in stasis, the viewer is caught between enjoyment of this empty passivity and the frustrated, unfulfilled desire to be given something to watch.

Warhol wrote that he filmed the way he did "because the more you look at the exact thing, the more the meaning goes away, and the better and emptier you feel."[4] He inspires a fundamental schism between the watcher and the watched. The film exists in order to have its meaning removed by the empty gaze of the viewer. Wollen describes this emptiness as the construction of "a mask, a shield, a screen which promise[s] immunity from the exchange of intersubjective looks, while permitting a whole economy of voyeurism and exhibitionism in the form of recorded spectacle."[5]

In *Poor Little Rich Girl* there is more action on-screen than in his earlier films but the relationship between the image and the viewer is still one of exclusion.[6] The camera sits in one place, and we must sit with it, while the actors wander around it, ignoring it and therefore ignoring us. The film is in focus for only a minute or so out of seventy and the rest of the time our voyeuristic pleasure in the image is denied. We are excluded from identification in two ways: by having our voyeurism frustrated because of the denied pleasure in the image that remains blurred, and by the fact that there is no plot underneath the blurred image that we could have latched onto, even if we had been allowed.

Warhol denies the viewer the ability to identify. He makes us empty ourselves during the length of the films, engendering an active sense of apathy akin to Sade's. While watching them in their full length, the audience is forced to battle silently between these two impulses. There is at once the response of the passive filmgoer trapped in a static peace during the film, and the active intellection of the filmgoer who struggles to process and forge identifications with the action on-screen. He makes us synthesize these two impulses, transforming active intellection into an emptiness that results in active apathy.

The principal force in Sade's writing is the pursuit of habitual transgression in crime. At the beginning of *Juliette*, Sade lays out his philosophy of apathy in a meeting between Juliette and a nun. Juliette is told that the act must first be completed and then it must be repeated until it has become habitual. The act, we discover, must be repeated until it is emptied of everything but the outrage that it signifies. The nun canonizes the criminal habit for the ways in which it obliterates the intensity of the act to the point where the act is performed apathetically. This principle is restated throughout his work. Sade's characters are made to struggle against values given to them by society, such as religion and morality. His characters must prove to themselves and each other that they can commit the most heinous crimes without suffering guilt or remorse over their actions. One must be able to prove that one has been able to renounce morality and develop the ability to conceive of and coldly carry out crimes more horrible than anyone else.

From this point, Sade sets out an alternative morality in which the detached pleasure taken in crime and cruelty represents the epitome of moral achievement. His characters flourish under this morality and are coldly ostracized or eliminated if they fail to take up new challenges in the pursuit of evil. They must engage in the project of emptying themselves of emotion through apathetic reiteration, excising common morality in order to replace it with the capacity to execute cold-blooded crimes. The apathy pursued in these works can be seen to represent the converse ideal to beatitude, as it is an active state of peace with oneself that arises from the ascesis of apathy through methods that mirror those used by saints in order to arrive at purity and holiness. Apathy becomes a method of distancing through which the self is placed outside of itself. The French theorist Pierre Klossowski states this process like this: "From the first time the act was committed, it presented itself as a promise of pleasure because its image was repellent. And if now the reiteration of the same act is to 'annihilate' conscience, it is because each time it is the same forces that, through their inversion, reestablish conscience. Inverted into a censorship, they will then provoke the act again."[7]

REPETITION

Both Warhol and Sade suppress significance through these methods of repetition. With these approaches in mind as the basic premises in their work, I will examine the writing/recording process as it mirrors these methods and synthesizes content with form, bringing us to an analysis of the way repetition and writing function together to transcend the representable. I will then explain the ways in which this repetition comes to mirror itself in the methods of portrayal.

Because Warhol becomes machinelike in order to repeat into nothingness, the act of repetition comes to represent the content of what is repeated. The portrayed and the portrayal become one. Warhol existed only as he recorded. He called his tape recorder his "wife" and was uncomfortable going anywhere without it. He regarded the telephone as the most intimate device ever invented and would talk on it for hours every day, recording every call. Using these strategies he maintained a separation between himself and the world, embracing it from the distance of voyeur. It is as though he had to witness his life through the camera in order to process it as experience.

In this way, what he records becomes the same as its repetition. Although his films consist of one long take without editing or retakes, his method is repetitive in that it marks the "making one" of life and its portrayal, thereby always repeating the life/portrayal that it shows. He removes the possibility of an event unwitnessed by the machine. In order to exist it must be recorded, and it is therefore "always already" repeated by its own representation.

What is irreducible in his experience becomes the whole. In contrast to the Hollywood filmmaking tradition, which reconstitutes the image through editing in an effort to make life more lifelike, Warhol reiterates the "unmediated" entirety.[8] For the artist-machine, apathy comes in the form of unmediated image: editing it would betray the mind behind the representation. He removes motivation from the act, representing only the act itself, and in doing so he offers the simulacrum of the act. Warhol arrives at the theatricalization of everyday life, transcending banality by celebrating it.

Similarly, Sade turns the act into the performance of that which is "always already" repeated. The relationship between doing and writing becomes an act of repetition that is identical for actor and reader. For Sade repetition is at the base of experience; it is through the act of writing—which depends on repetition—that the act is communicated. Sade's act of writing is comparable to the principle of the apathetic reiteration that he explores as a philosophy.

Klossowski writes: "The apathetic reiteration conveys Sade's own struggle to regain possession of what is irreducible in his experience . . . the actualization of the aberrant act by writing corresponds to the apathetic reiteration of this act itself perpetrated independently of its description."[9] Sade repeats the act by writing it, and when he writes, what he records is the act in pursuit of apathetic repetition. In this way, Sade's writing represents a deferred repetition in itself. Sade's act, which itself depends on its reiteration, becomes identical to the written reiteration of the act. For both Sade and Warhol the reiteration of the act *becomes* the act. I will go into this further by way of an analysis of transcendence in these texts in order to explain how their processes of writing reflect the unspeakable.

TRANSCENDENCE

In the process of slowing down a nonevent, as he does in his long, actionless films, Warhol takes the portrayal one extra step beyond the meaningful. He goes beyond what is shown in the portrayal of the event by emptying it and refusing audience identification. He leaves the viewer with a blank site upon which it is necessary to interpolate a meaning that is absent from the actual film. The content of the portrayal is removed and the audience is left to project its own interiority onto the performance: "the duration of the shot ensures . . . [that] if there is an effect of interiority it must come from elsewhere, from the spectator and his or her phantasmic mapping of self onto the image."[10] For Warhol, the object is repeated until it transcends what it shows. We end up looking beyond what is there. He shows us six hours of John Giorno sleeping at a speed that is actually slower than it is in reality, thereby repeating the language of film into nothingness.[11] He uses the process of recording nonevents to arrive at a level of the unspeakable. Warhol arrives at "the redemption of banality, the transcendence of the nausea of the replica, the volatile intermixing of sheer frivolity with passionate commitment, [in his] taste for excess and extravagance."[12] For Warhol, the repetition of the icon into nothingness becomes the celebration and transcendence of the object. For Sade, the repetition of the crime into nothingness becomes the celebration and transcendence of the crime.

The American performance artist Yvonne Rainer offers another example of the ways that Warhol and Sade repeat in order to transcend the content of their texts. In her 1963 piece, *Ordinary Dance*, Yvonne Rainer recites the tired concepts that delimit our experiences of relationships. She says, "I love you, I don't love you, I have never loved you."[13] She outlines the limits of expression and transcendence through the repetition that emerges from habit. By repeating these expressions in their banality, she explores that which is beyond the expressions themselves. Similarly, it is through an exaggeration of the familiarity of the erotic impulse that Sade arrives at a methodology that can transcend traditional boundaries and articulate the void that gives them their empty resonance. Sade gives us a grocery list of outrages whose every citation threatens the rational order. With the recitation of evils into meaninglessness, the sterile catalog that repeats in order to erase, the shock value recedes and all we are left with is a list.

Klossowski writes that Sade's acts are built around the incommunicable experience of ecstasy because the only way it can be portrayed is through repetition. It is his view that the representative element of Sade's discourse comes to show us what can only remain outside of it, through repetition and reiteration of the act: "This ecstasy cannot be conveyed by language; what language describes are the ways to it, the dispositions that prepare for it. But what does not get brought out clearly in Sade's conventional form of writing is that the ecstasy and the reiteration are the same thing." For the reader, "there remains only the reiteration described and the wholly exterior aspect of the ecstasy, the orgasm described, which is counterfeit ecstasy."[14]

For the viewer there is only parodied simulation—counterfeit ecstasy conveyed through the repetition of the act. With Warhol, through the process of watching *Sleep*, sleep is exteriorized. The experience is based on the reiteration of the act, which makes it accessible to the audience. We experience the event by experiencing its simulacrum. Warhol shows us a place where sleepers don't dream, where contemplative images don't think. The mechanized surfaces of the image-commodities are simulacra of the images we see: "Camp . . . with its hyperbolic aestheticism, its playful connaisseurship of kitch . . . was pushing insistently toward performance, toward the theatricalization of everyday life."[15] This is Warhol's counterfeit ecstasy. His images simulate the things they seem to represent. Warhol's films parody the ideas of active intellection and voyeuristic capacity. In *Lonesome Cowboys*,[16] Factory actors Tom Hompertz and Viva offer parody in place of seamless pornographic voyeurism: "and finally they start to fuck. I say fuck, but after a vigourous start Tom lies slumped at an angle while Viva thrusts her hips at a distance from his body which makes genital contact fairly implausible. It's neither simulated sex, nor simulated simulated sex, [it is] a parody of porn; Viva and Hompertz and Warhol suggest they can't even be bothered to go through the act of pretending."[17]

Klossowski locates the forever repeated transgression in the act of sodomy as it comprises the "key sign of all perversions."[18] The repetition of the fetishized act of sodomy is parallel to Warhol's repetition of the act because both construct a system of distancing through the elimination of conscience. Sade's sodomy is comparable to Warhol's camp because it becomes a minimalist act that depends on the detail, fetishizing outrage as Warhol's drag queen might fetishize the shoe. Klossowski writes: "Sodomy, from which sterile pleasure taken in a sterile object, experienced as a simulacrum of the destruction of norms, develops the Sadean emotion."[19] Klossowski situates Sade's simulacrum in the act of sodomy because the act itself can never be transgressed and is therefore presented each time as if it had never before been carried out.

TRANSGRESSION

Klossowski situates transgression in the act of distancing oneself from the crime. Sade's monster depends on the act of sodomy because it signifies the conscious transgression of the norms represented by conscience.[20] It is through the repetition of this act that the monster creates and maintains itself in his literature. Klossowski writes: "Monstrosity is the zone of this being outside of oneself, outside of conscience; the monster can maintain himself in this zone only by the reiteration of the same act."[21] Absence is embraced through reiteration in Sade, echoing Warhol's films and requiring the viewer to inject meaning into the vacancy on-screen. Just as Sade's monster depends on being outside of conscience, maintaining itself in the interstice between absence and presence through repetition, Warhol's machine depends on the empty repetition of simulacra in order to effectively remove the human element from the creation of the image.

Transgression inserts the aberrant act into rational discourse, and since Warhol and Sade both depend on logically structured language for expression, they must also transgress within discourse. But because they cannot actually transgress the laws they depend on, they reproduce the transgression within their discourses through repetition. Klossowski writes that Sade could apprehend the aberrant act "only in accordance with the laws of this language—by transgressing them. He never transgresses these laws except in the gesture whereby he reproduces them in their transgression."[22] Because the reiteration of outrage is inspired by the experience that is already structured by language, they restructure their logic around the aberrant act.

Since his approach is that of the machine that simply reproduces the event, Warhol's portrayal of the event is structured in advance by the experience itself. He is limited by the language of filmic representation because his cinema is one of tepid reproduction. Transgression of this language is parallel to Sade's in that the aberration cannot be described in the language of film so it is instead reproduced within it. Warhol mechanizes the image, removing as much as possible from its meaning. For him the aberrant act is related more closely to what is not there than to what is there. He leaves the empty shell of the unmotivated, uncritical image to stand in for the real. His image is a simulacrum because it no longer matters what is real and what is not: all is commodified, mechanized image. He transgresses the laws by leaving them to stand on their own without restructuring the experience according to the traditional laws of film, by reproducing without mediation: his authorship is as the artist-machine who records. Warhol outrages the logical structure of film by reproducing it without regard to traditional conventions: rather than breaking with convention he preserves it in order to transgress it through reproduction.[23]

Sade develops and systematizes the logical structure of language even in outraging it, "for he outrages it by conserving it only as a dimension of aberration—not because aberration is described in this logically structured language, but because the aberrant act is reproduced in it."[24] Sade subverts the logical structure of traditional language by constructing it as another dimension of aberration. In Sade the aberrant act is reproduced in the logically structured language but not described within it. In Warhol the aberrant act is the reproduction of the logically structured language without the reproduction of the rules that traditionally accompany the language and that normally structure the language of film. Both reproduce the act without describing it.

Warhol brings experience into the realm of frustrated voyeurism to be examined from a distance. By making performance and reality one he at once extends the private into the public sphere and publicizes the private sphere. Like Jorge Luis Borges's map, Warhol transcribes a universe on top of the existing one, blurring the distinction between them. Warhol's world is the frail, addicted understudy who stands in for the American cinema legend. Sade and Warhol present their worlds unmediated, imaginary, through writing.

Sade's bedroom "designates the bloody cave of the Cyclops, whose one eye is that of voracious thought."[25] In Warhol the eye of the Cyclops is a tiny mirror in a compact that is flipped open and carelessly held up for a time. If Sade's world becomes his boudoir, Warhol's boudoir becomes his world. The bedroom is the point from which experience extends into outside space, bringing experience of the bedroom out of the bedroom. These utopian spaces correspond to the ways the bedroom is specific yet transcendent. One might characterize these "utopias" as "ectopias," misplaced cells, separated, existing within circumstances that conspire to limit their growth. These "worlds" were never intended to grow to a size where they could stand on their own. By parodying themselves and the worlds that surround them, Warhol and Sade reject the utopian endeavor for its naïveté and are doomed from the first.

UTOPIAN SPACES

In the creation of their worlds, Sade and Warhol forge a separation from the "outside" that is at once significant for its difference and dependent on its otherness to the mainstream culture it opposes. I refer to Warhol's world of the Factory in order to explore the specificity of the situation he created, and take this specific reference point as a way of placing his utopia in a literal space for the purposes of analysis. Similarly, I am placing the universe that Sade created in his literature within the dungeon/boudoir, because the separation he imposes and explores in his philosophy is significant insofar as it depends on being representable within a hidden, enclosed space. I will examine the ways in which the creation of these spaces represents the articulation of the underside, the unknown, and the way they constitute and are constituted by theories of the "other."

Sade constructs sacred/profane spaces such as the castle, the dungeon, the boudoir, and the estate in which he situates his characters. His characters operate within these spaces as refugees from the outside world, adopting a fantasy function where morality is suspended in favor of the pursuit of cold criminal activity. Every space he enters in the role of his characters is a closed area, whether it is a convent or monastery in which he delights in the placement of libertines in ecclesiastical robes, or inside the regular venues of his main characters, such as Juliette's estate, into which she draws unsuspecting victims. The only reason Juliette has to venture out of her estate is in search of new blood to spill. Every scene is located within the walls of his distinct, criminal space. The outside world is thus posited as something to rebel against; Sade reconstructs outer society as the domain of the unenlightened peasant class who cannot arrive at libertinage because of their own inadequacy. Sade's kingdom becomes this self-imposed confined area in which morality can be bled, sodomized, or tortured into silence. This space is dependent on the walls that enclose it from outside forces; it becomes a haven, a refuge from common morality where the focus is placed on the pursuit of apathy.

Once the governing idea becomes one of enclosure, a sense of restriction is implied. The delimited space becomes a metaphor for the ascesis of apathy marking the character's pursuit of emptiness. The characters are involved in a metaphorical self-discipline that corresponds to the outer walls of the estate: they hold ethics at bay in order to pursue empty transgressions behind closed doors. They construct the walls of the castle in order to bar the morality of the outside world from their sacred/profane space, confining themselves in order to remain separate from the world and to pursue transgression as an operative principle. This space is then self-contained, posited in relation and in opposition to the outside world. It comes to represent a tiny cell of "otherness" that is sheltered from the outside lest it become sullied through acts of charity or piety. It is a twisted morality in which evil must be kept pure, as delicate and honest a pursuit as the pursuit of spiritual purity through selfless acts or the ascesis of sainthood.

The characters are privileged with the freedom to wander out into the world of morality in order to seek out new crimes and new victims. They are granted a sort of transcendence by virtue of their wealth that allows them to remain enclosed within their walls as a luxury of separation rather than as a penance. This is another way in which Sade twists morality, reviewing the context of prison to include the concealed and the secret as luxuries that emerge from the impunity of the characters. He parodies the prison, turning it inside out so that its punishments come to represent desire.

The freedom of the characters is directly connected to the luxury they are granted to exist within their dungeons. It is in being removed from their castles that they become vulnerable. I am reminded here of a particular segment in *Juliette* where she and Clarewil are kidnapped as they travel from their estate.[26] They are being held until the family they murdered the night before is proven to be alive, and freed. Here the castle becomes a prison, but Juliette and Clarewil are able to transform the rules of the prison/castle over to their own rules, thereby escaping punishment. In the end, they set someone else up for the original crime and commit another on top of the first, seducing and then murdering their guards. They are able to subvert the prison structure in such a way as to restore the rules of their self-imposed prison, demonstrating a comfort in the prison structure that comes from having spent all their time enclosed in one that is self-imposed. Transcendence and subversion result from having learned to adopt and reassert the traditional signifiers of punishment toward sexual fulfilment and empowerment. They succeed in transcending the stigma of punishment, thereby regrouping that same stigma in their own context and subverting it by taking pleasure in the despicable. They turn the signifiers of torture into signifiers of pleasure and transgression.

INVERSION AND CARNIVAL

Like Sade's castle/dungeon/boudoir, Warhol's Factory is a haven in the midst of an outside culture. Warhol parodies the nature of industrial production by positing his Factory as a site of consumption, a site where the working class is suppressed in favor of a perverse bohemian ideal based on consumption and repetition. It is a deflective/reflective dungeon with tinfoil wallpaper, a naïvely monstrous house of mirrors inside of which values are inverted. The world inside the Factory walls becomes a carnival where fool becomes king for fifteen minutes.

The factory and the dungeon/boudoir construct an arena of reversal within their separate spaces that is reminiscent of Mikhail Bakhtin's notion of carnival. Warhol's Factory located itself outside of the standards of industrial production, overhauling traditional modes of production for parodic purposes. The Factory reconstructs a world in which the prohibitions and restrictions that govern the industrial paradigm are suspended, where an alternate universe comes to life. The Factory, like the dungeon/boudoir, separates in order to parody and suspend the standards of the culture inside of which it is bracketed. The traditional forms of social hierarchy are overturned inside these spaces in a way that links them to carnival, temporarily transgressing and reversing order. Inside these carnivalistic spaces eccentricity and distance are exalted and apathy becomes the dominant force: "As theatrical representation, it abolishes the dividing line between performers and spectators, since everyone becomes an active participant and everyone communes in the carnival act, which is neither contemplated nor, strictly speaking, performed; it is lived."[27] Performance becomes life within the paradigm of camp. Carnival unifies the sacred with the profane, the significant with the insignificant, the original with the copy.

This suspension of social hierarchy is evident in Sade as it marks Sade's rejection of religion and ethics in place of a reconstructed hierarchy based on atheism and the criminal habit. Warhol overturns the mainstream by exalting marginality and eccentricity, offering burlesque in place of law, campy performance in place of life. Within their walls the outside world is inverted.

Warhol's world is based around this fusion of opposites in every respect. He addresses metropolitan anonymity and its converse dependence on fame. His Factory represents the meeting of the fashionable with the underground, where urban marginality is introduced to high fashion, where debutantes and hustlers merge in a mad celebration of the inversion of outside norms.

The key signifier of this inversion in Bakhtin's terms is the "crowning and subsequent decrowning of the carnival king."[28] This concept is manifest in a scene in *The Chelsea Girls* where Factory denizen Ondine crowns himself pope in order to illustrate Warhol's carnival kingdom.[29] He shoots up, settles back, and begins hearing "confessions" from the other people present. At the climax he addresses a girl who admits she is reluctant to give her confession because she sees him as a "phony." He blows up and begins to slap her violently. Her line of questioning introduces a fissure into the carnival canon. Ondine's reign as pope is over because he has lost his head and because by refusing the carnival inversion the woman has launched a "radical assault upon the Factory's regime of representation and, by implication, upon its spatiotemporal axis."[30]

The unwritten rule in Warhol's universe requires an absolute surface orientation: to get "really" anything is not allowed. An absolute veneer of "cool" detachment must remain in place, even through the festivities of the carnival. "Real" emotion is prohibited in favor of removed apathy. Emotion and skepticism of the carnival order must be suspended within Warhol's emptied sphere. When Ondine explodes he is forced to admit defeat and step down from popedom because he has broken Warhol's unwritten rule. The carnival king has been crowned and decrowned.

Sade's carnival crowning inverts itself within almost every scene. Sade consistently presents us with a central figure of libertinage who takes control over the proceedings, choosing his victims, then flippantly sodomizing and murdering them. In turn, the "king" is himself sodomized in a Bakhtinian reversal that is akin to Ondine's reign as pope.

DEATH AND RENEWAL

The notion of carnival as it revolves around the cycle of death and renewal brings us to an analysis of the symbolic deaths in Warhol and this sense of renewal and annihilation in Sade. Warhol's symbolic death comes in the interstice between script and conversation. The script is present in order to be denied, as it is the performance of spontaneous action in which Warhol is interested. In his film *Kitchen*, a group of people is framed within a gleaming white kitchen filled with appliances.[31] In the film, everyone goes off into detached monologues, and Edie Sedgewick takes out a fork and begins to roast a marshmallow over the stove. The kitchen table in the center of the frame is used for various things during the length of the film, but now it is cleared off in order to make space for the murder. Edie is placed on the table, unresisting, and strangled. She sits up and protests that she has burned her finger on the fork. Someone goes to get a Band-Aid. The crew enters the set and for the next few minutes everyone surrounds her, offering her various remedies for the burn. Her scripted death corresponds to the symbolic death of the script. By sitting up and protesting, she completes the death of the script and inspires the renewal of spontaneous action. This is what Warhol wanted to film in the first place. It is through the removal of form that his form emerges.

In his rejection of God and his subsequent exaltation of nature, Sade summons the active power in nature that destroys in order to strengthen. Indeed, his characters, in their cycles of desire, orgasm ("little deaths"), and exhaustion, take their strength from killing. Minski, the Russian ogre in *Juliette*, eats his victim's flesh and extols the virtues of its power to restore strength after the tiring cycle of orgasm and sacrifice. The fact that he makes a point of eating his latest victims for dinner introduces Sade's central idea of inverting the procreative facility toward a notion of consumption. Production (procreation) in Sade is overturned by consumption. Similarly, Warhol absorbs the paradigm of capitalist production and celebrates the consequent fixation on consumption.

Warhol's Factory parodies the factory as the site of industry, internalizing the tension in capitalism that rests on the cycle of production and consumption. The production/creation vs. consumption/destruction correspondences are inverted: Warhol destroys what he produces by ripping consumer images out of context, destroying their given meanings by reproducing them in the context of the factory. And he consumes what he creates by laying his Borgesian map on top of the existing world, offering recorded images as emptied shadows to be watched, consumed, and forgotten. (He never watched his films after they were shot. He put them away in unlabelled boxes and sent them to New Jersey.) Conversely, his creations celebrate consumption. He commodifies the images he produces and markets them as items for consumption. The dualism between production/creation and consumption/destruction is further confounded as he is created by that which he consumes. Consumption comes to represent the lack of closure in the subject constituted through the always unfulfilled desire to consume.

By escalating the American dream of consumption to a nightmare pace, Warhol articulates the death drive that exists on the underside of culture, forever repeating itself by offering more and more commodities. Warhol's benign soup cans are necessarily accompanied by the contaminated tuna in his *Tuna Fish Disaster.* Or, in the words of Thierry de Duve, "One doesn't take on the existence of a thing of absolute narcissism without drawing pleasure out of that which drove Marilyn to suicide."[32] By assuming the role of the recording machine, Warhol implicitly enters into the role of the killing machine: he is camera and car crash, tape recorder and electric chair.

Hierarchy is always implicitly twisted in Sade. He is always positing the criminal as king and the king as criminal. He takes the "respectable" elements of outer society (priests, aristocrats, nuns) and transforms them into libertines. He simultaneously documents the ascent of his libertines (Juliette) to higher positions in society as they steal money and do favors for other aristocratic libertines until they come to possess an unassailable financial and social power, the direct result of criminal achievement. Sade constantly usurps the order of outside society in favor of his own hierarchy. He joyously rejects the "natural" deferral to authority and common taboos in favor of his uniquely twisted order, evidence of which is especially apparent in Juliette's act of incest and her subsequent parricide. This inversion articulates the rejection of ethical authority in the absence of God.

"ANTIHEROES" AND THE BODY

Warhol's Factory people are parallel to Sade's libertines: they are a group of like-minded outcasts who deify their marginality through the pursuit of perverse and contrary paradigms as delineated by the auteur. They are drug addicts, homosexuals, drag queens, malcontent "society girls": people whose operation in outside society is marginalized in the New York of the 1960s. It is this marginalization that impels them toward

Warhol's universe, where they are liberated behind Factory walls, loosed within his closed off society where deviance is the norm. It is the goal to which they aspire, the place where they become stars of anti-Hollywood and icons of perverse freedom.

Like Sade's libertines who subvert the prison, Warhol parodies the Hollywood system. He once said that he was interested in the "stars of the out take"; the one girl out of a hundred in an Esther Williams movie who doesn't jump off the swing at the cue and ends up on the cutting room floor.[33] He parodies Hollywood cinema, filming on the underside in a way that breaks with Hollywood instead of breaking away from it. Warhol's films, for example, contrast with the abstract experimental films of Michael Snow, who signalled a total refusal of Hollywood cinema by abandoning the star system, narrative cinema, and the voyeuristic impulse. In *So It Is* Snow gives us only text on a black background, removing every vestige of the spectacle. Instead of employing this kind of fissure, Warhol celebrates the Hollywood spectacle, retaining its format in order to pervert it.

He parodies the star system by investing his misfits with celebrity and by presenting his superstars lying around in bed talking nonsense rather than exuding glamour and mystery. He parodies narrative by collapsing it, presenting the audience with eight hours of the Empire State Building in order to fuse art and life. In *Empire* he critiques Hollywood's editing process, which dissects life in order to make it more "lifelike."[34] Warhol exploits and explodes the visual element of film, perverting the traditional narrative format by imitating it in marvellous camp theater. When the sleeping man twitches, we are absorbed: arbitrary actions replace plot developments in the absence of plot. His films have everything to do with the entertainment film industry but they approach it via the deflective tinfoil walls of the Factory, where America's outtake is canonized, thereby reaffirming both the intake and the subversion of the system that produced it.

Behind Factory walls Warhol is at once separate from the world and at its center. The Factory, surrounded by the American urban experience and the consumer culture whose icons Warhol adopts and manufactures, remains a closed off space. For its coherence, the Factory depends on the contrast between itself and the rest of the world. The Factory is his utopia where he can be hedged with the protection of "his" people, and it is his dystopia where he cannot disappear, where instead he is centralized. He adopts the trappings of consumer culture and celebrates

them in the process of subverting them. At the same time that he celebrates fame and the Hollywood star system he retains enigma, remaining untouchable. He fuses fame with anonymity, high art with low art,
Hollywood spectacle with pornography, narrative with *cinema verité*, and
cinema verité with camp spectacle. Warhol is unified by the alienation
that emerges from the desire to consume. He is constituted through
alienation and the lack of closure that represents desire.

The world revolves around detached desire. In *The Thirteen Most
Beautiful Women* the frame rests on thirteen women who vacuously
stare into the camera, one by one, department store mannequins of the
undead.[35] There is a tension between intensity and absence in their
gazes. Warhol's subject is composed through this sense of incompletion
that is alienation and the capitalist desire to consume. His thirteen women
are reduced to surface and presented as commodities unto themselves:
they are products manufactured in the factory. The Factory celebrates
the capitalist system, twists it, and extends it into meaninglessness.

The Factory is dependent on what is outside of its text in order to
be defined. It needs the "other" in order to exist. They can only exist by
being "othered" by mainstream culture, requiring marginality in order
to be distinct. They embrace their alienation, only constituted as subjects insofar as they are incomplete. Completion is always deferred
because the missing piece is always pursued but never attained. In a
spiralling tension between appearance and disappearance, the missing
piece is projected from the factory or the dungeon onto the outside culture, and then re-presented back into the microcosm. They want to
appear, they want to disappear. They want to exist, they want to dissolve
into nothingness. Like the Egyptian mummies, they need to be hidden
in order to appear.

The same tension between appearance and disappearance that is
evident in Warhol's enigmatic celebrity is present in an analysis of Sade
as a pariah figure. In order to write he is exiled into the dungeon. Com-
mitting the criminal act (in real life) results in his disappearance into the
prison, where he appears through his writing. To appear he must disappear; to write he must have committed the acts that exiled him.

Sade projects himself into the healthy perverted bodies of his characters, whereas Warhol projects himself into bodies of exquisite sickness. Sade explicitly portrays the bodies of his victims as being "perfect
specimens" in order to emphasize the contrast between the victim before
and after the criminal act. His pleasure is in the transference of healthy

bodies into the violated corpses that are the by-product of his criminal act. Sade projects healthy bodies to be desecrated. Warhol projects beautiful, sickly bodies to be celebrated.

Warhol's bodies are addicted bodies, perverse bodies, transvestite bodies, emaciated amphetamine bodies that articulate deferred subjectivity. Warhol places these lost denizens of the Factory in front of the camera where they loiter in languid catatonia, oblivious to us. There is a sense of helpless empathy that combines with voyeuristic fascination when we see that they are beautiful because of the way they are dying. We realize that the reasons we have to see them are directly related to the specificity of their destruction. In this aspect, Sade and Warhol provide us with the same functional captivation with sickness and death for pleasure.

The difference between the voyeuristic capacities explored in Sade's literary sex crimes and Warhol's films is one of timing. We are hypnotized by the act of watching Warhol's people engage in the most phantasmic of everyday activities: we are invited to witness the fatuous decline of bodies from a time that defined itself in view of its extinction. The viewer is absorbed by the spectacle of these vacuous people filling themselves with pharmaceuticals, staring out at us and lounging around in bed in a drugged-out stupor. In *Poor Little Rich Girl* we see Edie Sedgewick pace in between the bed and the telephone; Amphetamine Barbie in leopard print underwear. During the film we are aware, as she could not have been, that we are watching haunted shadows of imminent death. We are trapped in this soporific universe without motivation, entranced by his brand of painful beauty. Warhol captures us with a sad, sick fascination because he reflects the seductive phantoms of the factory. These actors, whose lives have been fused with performance, are victims whose sacrifice is refused, deferred. Sade shows us the death of his victims but Warhol has infinitely more impact by giving us bodies that are fascinating for their weakness and their fragile, perverse beauty. We participate in their drugged-out stardom. They are dynamic, yet paralyzed; they create a maelstrom with their anomaly, drawing us in. They die later, in anonymity, away from Warhol's camera, in many cases as a result of the weaknesses that made them so fascinating to watch in their heyday. Edie Sedgewick died in 1971 from a barbiturate overdose, sacrificed to the anti-Hollywood Warhol had fabricated. And if the rest of them do not die plush amphetamine deaths, the Factory crew suffers a symbolic death of anonymity once the Factory has dissipated. The narrative ends with the decline of Warhol's Factory empire because it existed in the first place in a separate utopian moment.

CONCLUSION

The similarities between the work of Warhol and Sade are aligned with repetition in philosophy and method. An analysis of apathetic repetition is necessary for an understanding of the ways their approaches intersect because it is the fundamental principle that guides their work. Although Warhol and Sade are different in many ways, apathetic reiteration brings them together in order to facilitate a rejection of the societal values that surround them. They both seize the central values of their societies in order to construct perverse antitheses to them as guiding principles within their separate realms. In Sade's time it was perhaps religion, with all of its attendant sexual taboos, that constructed the essential societal norm his atheism rebelled against through outrage. For Warhol, perhaps the centrality of the celebrity and the schism between high and low art are the essential values he perverts when he reconstructs himself as a machine, and produces art within the same framework that relentlessly produces frivolous commodities. Sade and Warhol are ultimately social critics: they construct their worlds in order to critique and parody outside values. For Sade the critique is performed through outrage, for Warhol it is performed in a trance designed to refuse meaning. They parody the utopian concept in order to set themselves in secret realms where the values they depend on for coherence are inverted. By focusing on the underside of "no-place/good-place," they simultaneously situate themselves in imaginary spaces where their philosophies are lived out in isolation, and reject the utility of the utopian endeavor by refusing to construct idyllic, unproblematic spheres of existence. Their "utopias" specifically concentrate on the incomplete nature of desire and therefore are not utopias at all. They refuse the idea of a world in which everything is unproblematic and focus on the necessity of conflict for happiness. It is only this aspect of their worlds that becomes utopian, as temporary satiation leading to further outrage is part of the transgressive enterprise pursued through repetition as a basic principle in their work.

Chapter Two

Kierkegaard, History, and Modern Art

IN THIS CHAPTER I WILL ANALYZE Søren Kierkegaard's account of history, time, figuralism, and repetition with reference to modern art. It is my intention to look at abstract art's search to represent the unrepresentable as having parallels to Kierkegaard's task of imagining the unimaginable. I will draw a parallel between Kierkegaard's condition of possibility (God) and the modern notion of the "act of existence" (indirectly, Heidegger's *das Ereignis*) in order to place these notions in relation to the art of Barnett Newman, Ad Reinhardt, and Kasimir Malevich, who attempt to express "man's natural desire for the exalted" by silently gesturing toward the transcendental signified.[1]

What I am calling "the project of abstraction" is the project of removing the inessential in the realm of representation in order to arrive at the essential, or, to put it another way, to derive the universal from the particular. It is the stripping away of contingent figurations (the many) to arrive at the transcendent One.[2] Because abstraction explores representability in order to address the possibility of the existence of the unrepresentable, I am led to draw a parallel between it and the fundamental inexpressibility of the "other," or creative activity, that functions at the center of many philosophies.

Whether this creative activity is conceived of as the pre-Socratic infinite, the Neoplatonic One, the Christian creator-God, the philosophical notion of the act of existence, Heidegger's *das Ereignis*, or Lacan's Real, the function is the same: to explore the limit at the edge of human experience in order to glimpse that which is the condition of existence. These notions arise in response to the questions "Why is there anything? What is the nature and source of creativity?" As Jean

Francois Lyotard writes of Barnett Newman, "He breaks with the eloquence of romantic art but does not reject its fundamental task, that of bearing pictorial or otherwise expressive witness to the inexpressible. The inexpressible does not reside in an over there, in another work, or another time, but in this: *that something happens.* In the determination of pictorial art, the indeterminate, the 'it happens' is the paint, the picture. The paint, the picture as occurrence or event, is not expressible, and it is to this that it has to witness."[3]

The "something" that "happens" refers to the act of existence. This is the condition of existence in which the "act of existence" refers to that activity by virtue of which a thing is what it is. I will compare the modern notion of the act of existence with Kierkegaard's God in order to determine the respective functions of the inexpressible "other" in Kierkegaard's texts and modern art. It is my assertion that God and the modern notion of the act of existence have everything in common except their relation to the infinite, because for Kierkegaard God is infinite, whereas modern act is defined as finite.[4] This is not as big a difference as it may seem, however, because they function the same way regardless of the difference. It is my opinion that Kierkegaard's ultimate relationship to God (in the religious stage) results in a focus on the finite realm because his God is totally "other" and must therefore ultimately function as that which is "beyond" the limit of comprehension, the same way representation works for the abstract artists.

Kierkegaard's God is a transcendent, markless unity from which all things emerge. The basis of his theory is his account of "coming-into-being," which defines the way he thinks of the silent mystery of existence, God the "other." He is adamant that reason cannot encompass the nature of God. Similarly, the abstract expressionists seek "immediate union with the Real" by abstracting away from signifiers in order to reveal the "presence of the transcendental signified."[5] Kierkegaard attempts to strip away markers of the human in order to arrive at the (markless) "other" of God just as the abstract expressionists strip away signifiers in order to glimpse the "Real."

Kierkegaard asks us to imagine the unimaginable: union with the "other" that can only be manifest in the relation with God. He silently points to the unimaginable in two ways. First, he explicitly gestures to God throughout his texts because God lies at the center of his project.

The religious stage of existence requires the individual to grasp God first through submission and then by grasping the absurdity endemic to the notion of union with such a totality. The individual undergoes a struggle to achieve union with God, a struggle that can only be alluded to by pointing silently at the divine realm. To grasp the infinite is to live fully in the finite, and to understand the finite is to achieve union with the infinite. For Kierkegaard freedom is paradoxically found in bondage in the face of the fullness of God.

Kierkegaard's silent gesture also functions underneath the text by pointing to what cannot be expressed through language. He employs indirection in his writing project, a methodology in which circularity functions to reveal as it withdraws, constantly pointing away from one text to another until the reader is led to the limit of language. He does this partly by writing pseudonymously and in fragments that function like Nietzsche's aphorisms, and partly by parodying the philosophical tract itself, as is the case in *Repetition: An Essay in Experimental Psychology*, which adopts a semifictional stance in order to divert the reader from his/her traditional placement in relation to the philosophical text. He confounds the relationship between the text and the reader by constructing a complex play of identification that ultimately retreats from expression, leaving the trace of the gesture to the inexpressible. In both senses this gesture is the admission that there is an Inexpressible, whether it lies above and beyond the human realm in the form of God or beyond the limits of language. These are points that will addressed more closely in the section on limit. Here I would like to direct the analysis toward an examination of Kierkegaard's philosophy itself in order to lay the foundation for later points.

KIERKEGAARD UNPLUGGED

As we have seen, Kierkegaard's God is a transcendent, markless, "other" entity that is the condition for existence. In his philosophical system, the act of "coming-into-being" is a result of the intervention of God upon a "manifold possibility" that results in the conversion of this possibility into actuality. For Kierkegaard, becoming is the result of the incursion of actuality into the realm of possibility through divine intervention.

The actual and the possible are discontinuous, and while the possible remains radically indeterminate, it "clings to"[6] the actual, which functions as the basic component of existence.[7]

Kierkegaard maintains that becoming is a contingent, nonnecessary process that is the result of the intervention of God. God enters the moment when actuality interacts with possibility, thereby bringing something into being.[8] In order to retain what he sees as essential for freedom, Kierkegaard insists that the causes that produce freedom are nonlogical and nonsystematic.

By focusing on the moment of divine intervention in the process of becoming, Kierkegaard focuses on the radical individuality of the object. The contingency and uniqueness of each act of "coming-into-being" prompts Kierkegaard to assert the singularity of each event of becoming, and the "wonderment" of the individual object. The movement from possibility to "concrete singularity" remains an essential notion for him as it lays the foundation for his theory of history. He writes: "The historicity of the past consists in its having once been present through having come into existence."[9]

Kierkegaard's history emerges from the role of divine intervention in the historical continuum. Although he defines history as a linear process, by leaving open the possibility for interventions from God he insists that history is not wholly rational or accessible to pure reason. This combination gives rise to his theory of repetition, which breaks the continuity of linear time by divine intervention yet allows for events that are connected only insofar as they prefigure and repeat each other.[10]

In Kierkegaard's system, change is figural. His theory of time asserts a linearity to history, yet also retains the notion of God's intervention at various points so as to confound any conception of a historical system that is accessible to pure reason or an overarching principle of explanation. History is structured not by logical systems but by the recurrence of familiar structures. His basis for repetition lies in medieval readings of biblical text: allegorical and anagogical readings of the Bible that cast the Messiah as a figure whose entry into the historical continuum changes everything, both past and future, by virtue of its nature.

Allegorical readings of the Bible look back on some events as prefigurations of other events, casting, for example, prophets and messengers in the Old Testament as prefigurations of Jesus. Anagogical readings cast the Bible in terms of the future because it holds that the things written in the Bible will be ratified through salvation and prophecy. As a Christian, Kierkegaard holds the theory that Jesus is the paradigm example of the insertion of the divine into the historical continuum, the universal into the particular. He then uses this as the basis for his theory regarding the passage of history. Kierkegaard links the two modes of biblical interpretation in his own conception of repetition, because for him structures are repeated forward rather than backward and represent the reinsertion of familiar structures at various points in history, changing the way their recurrence is seen each time they reappear.

The point of Kierkegaard's emphasis on the Messiah as an injection of the universal into the particular is that the repetition of this structure goes on in the course of the becoming of any object, since his world works from the universal toward the particular in all cases. The Messiah is the model for the "leap into being" that characterizes the conversion of possibility into actuality at the point of transition. It is in this way that Kierkegaard accounts for all nonimmanent movement and genuine change. Therefore repetition is the function by which genuine change is brought about. The question of novelty arises in this regard: how is genuine change brought about through repetition if by definition repetition means that which is not new?

Kierkegaard's answer to this is that because the relationship between actuality and possibility is discontinuous and nonnecessary, every incarnation is novel simply by being reinserted into the historical continuum. Novelty is not in itself significant for Kierkegaard; instead the emergence of familiar structures attains absolute significance. The changes that emerge are neither new nor old; they are simply different, and therefore novelty has no place. Each incarnation/emergence changes both what came before and what will come in the future, as each irruption into the historical continuum creates difference.

The notion of repetition is crucial to Kierkegaard's theory of history. By insisting on the possibility of divine intervention in the creation of things, and by using the Incarnation as a model for the impetus that drives history forward, Kierkegaard stresses the importance of the repetitive structures that are refigured in the course of history. Kierkegaard does not mean that the Messiah is the only structure that is repeated, but rather that the injection of the universal into the particular historical continuum by God is the model for the progression of history toward salvation. For Kierkegaard, repetition repeats into the future, functioning the same way that Christian history does, that is anagogically, by looking toward future salvation. He holds that the only possible goal to which history is driven is the future salvation of the individual, on a nonnecessary, solitary path to the religious stage of existence. If one sees Kierkegaard's God as functioning the same way as the finite act of existence, repeated structures may be interpreted more broadly than is implied by the Incarnation example.

What I would like to do with the notions of figuralism and repetition in this regard is to reinterpret figuralism by tracing the emergence and reemergence of structures in the realm of qualitative difference rather than in the realm of absolute significance. The difference of God for Kierkegaard is absolute, as God is unimaginably "other." Because the act of existence is finite, the difference that emerges from it is qualitative, a series of differences rather than the (absolute) Difference. I will look at this in my analysis of the repetitive and figuralist structures as they are manifest in the art of the New York School. Here I will outline my points regarding the similarities between Kierkegaard and modern art.

First, I will look at the pertinence of repetition and figuralism to both projects. Second, I will look at issues related to the limit in order to consider the ways both abstraction and faith wrestle with the intersection that divides the human and the divine, the representable and the unrepresentable. Next I will examine the ways in which these projects seek union with God or equivalent; and finally I will consider Kierkegaard's religious stage of existence in order to place it in relation to the sublime responsibility that emerges from the human experience of God. The last three points will be tied together in a synthesis of issues emerging from the limit of unrepresentability and unspeakability.

THE ART PART

In order to tie these points about repetition and figuralism to modern art I will provide a bit of history about these painters and projects. Kasimir Malevich (1878–1935) was a Russian artist painting from around 1903 to 1920. Although in the course of his career he worked through a number of styles—impressionism, symbolism, primitivism, futurism, and cubism—I am primarily concerned with those works that fall under the aegis of "suprematist" art, that is, art that seeks to "define and extend

[the] new formal vocabulary, or to represent feelings."[11] In particular, I am concerned with his painting *Black Square*.

In 1915 he exhibited *Black Square* at the 0.10 exhibition in Petrograd, where he hung it in the upper corner of the room that is traditionally reserved for the religious icon in the homes of Russian Orthodox believers. Its placement is significant; Malevich's *Black Square*, I will demonstrate, is an attempt to represent the "transcendental signifier," i.e., the figuration of the "absent presence" of the transcendent God.

During this phase he experimented with many squares, painting white-on-white, black-on-white, and black-on-black canvases. Primarily the works were squares revolving within and around the space of the canvas, extending the represented space by extending the shape of the square beyond the edge of the canvas. This extensivity is interesting for two reasons. First, his black-on-black works look into an "origin," which is why I see their congruence with Ad Reinhardt's black paintings. Secondly, his revolving squares, by extending the frame of the canvas (itself a square), delimits the traditionally representable space and results in the creation of a spiral at once inward (to the center of the painting, where there is no detail that would betray its reason for drawing the viewer in) and outward (past the outer limits of the canvas into the world, in a spiraling, recursive structure that has no logical end).

Ad Reinhardt (1913–1967) was an American painter associated with the New York School. Reinhardt painted his series of black paintings between 1954 and 1967, almost forty years after Malevich's *Black Square*. Reinhardt's black paintings consisted of black-on-black rectangles inscribed with almost invisible (black) geometric sections overlapping the field of the canvas. His paintings, however, differ from Malevich's in that they are an attempt to paint the "last painting," because Reinhardt saw abstraction as the final step before the end of art. The interesting thing here is that during the course of his attempts to paint the "last painting," Reinhardt produced a series of black paintings that ended up differing subtly from one to the next, with different shadings and gradations between them. In his black series he removes and then reinstates the repressed figure of a cross that, like Malevich's square, is barely visible, yet undeniably present at the center. To attempt to paint the last painting, Reinhardt had to paint it over and over again: he had to repeat the project until the figuration he had initially attempted to eliminate reemerged in a slightly varied form.

The abstract expressionist painter Barnett Newman (1905–1970), also of the New York School, differs significantly from both Malevich and Reinhardt. His paintings are generally huge, with stripes running across or down vast segments of monochrome canvas. For my purposes here I am referring to Newman's all-black *Primordial Light* (1954), the single inverse stripe of *Abraham* (1949), and the *Onement* series (1949), which are elongated, black canvases with one stripe running down the length of the middle. *Onement* is a theoretically infinite series, as "One-ment" extends forever: the constantly deferred presence of the "Real" "One."

REPETITION AND FIGURALISM

In this section I will look at the attempt of abstract art to refigure the repetitive emergence of the God-equivalent, repetition as it functions between certain paintings and projects, figuration as it is equivalent to figuralism in regard to the act, and the limits of representation as they evolve through repetition.

It is tempting to cast the abstract artists' search to represent the "origin" as an attempt to figure an origin that is somehow prehistori-cal.[12] It is more accurate, however, to view their project as being the attempt to explore creativity itself; the finite act of creativity from which all things emerge. This sense of the act is not prehistorical in the least: if anything, it is more accurately described as transhistorical, the attempt to figure the condition of figuring itself.

Abstraction ultimately emerges from the finite realm because the "act of existence" is ongoing in that it operates in and through the finite realm at all times. It is my idea here that notions of the "origin" in modern art effectively represent a reversal of the Jesus figure, an attempt to refigure the repetitive emergences of the God-equivalent in history, in that the act moves from the particular to the universal (the human to the divine) instead of moving from the universal to the particular, as in the model of the Incarnation. Abstraction effectively reverses movement away from the infinite to the finite, from the impetus of an infinite God to the principle of finite creativity.

This brings me to the parallel between Kierkegaard's Incarnation (figuralism) and repetition in abstract expressionism. Since I am drawing this analysis on the basis of the artists' injection of qualitative difference into history rather than Kierkegaard's absolute difference inserted by the divine into historical linearity, I see the emergence and reemergence of similar themes between paintings (as they emerge from the free act) as an echo of Kierkegaard's irruptions of the divine into historical linearity. This is the basis for my analysis of the paintings as instances of repetition.

Repetition functions between works in a series by one artist (as in Newman's *Onement* series), between different artists in what they achieve or attempt (as between Malevich's *Black Square* and Reinhardt's black paintings), and in the theoretical impetus behind all these artists that results in varied yet uncannily similar conclusions about the status of representation, lending their individual journeys as artists a Kierkegaardian air of solitude and struggle through repetition.

In a Kierkegaardian sense, these repetitions are significant because of the discontinuous chronological effect that they represent. The appearance and reappearance of the black canvases between Moscow (Malevich) and New York (Reinhardt) after an absence of several decades introduced a new set of conditions for the black canvases. Malevich's *Black Square* and Reinhardt's black paintings mean different things despite the fact that they look so similar. The reemergence of the black paintings of Reinhardt and Malevich in different contexts echoes the figuralist notion in Kierkegaard with the difference that the repetition is about qualitative difference instead of the absolute significance of the Incarnation. The different ways these black paintings reappear reveal that their contextual shifts require that they approach and retreat from meaning as the bounds of meaning change with each "incarnation." A particularly overt example of this can be seen within Malevich's squares themselves. After a lengthy period of complete nonproductivity at the end of his career, Malevich returned to his black square. In an effort to cash in on his initial success he dated these late canvases back to his early period. By the time the "black square" reemerged it was functioning as a simulacrum of Malevich's early attempt to represent the unrepresentable.

Because the acts of the artist (in a Kierkegaardian framework) cannot be viewed in terms of cause and effect but are instead individual free acts of becoming, repetition in art is a process that runs parallel to the reemergence of the Messiah's "lost figure" in the course of history. The refiguration of acts is a nonnecessary, free, and individual process.

The black paintings bring in repetition as the canvases represent the reintroduction of a lost figure (or, in this case, lost nonfigure) into the historical continuum. They insert difference each time they are painted, throwing everything before and after them into different relations each time they appear.

These abstract painters begin with the initial premise that figuration is inessential and must be stripped away in order to approximate the essential mystery of the condition of being.[13] Their figures become twisted and repressed (Malevich's crosses), abstracted until the figures themselves are stripped to their essential core (Newman's "zips" dividing the canvas) or silently reappear in the repetition of their absence (as for the figure of the cross, which disappears and reemerges in the course of Reinhardt's black paintings).

Figuration is the representational equivalent of figuralism. Kierkegaard's reinsertion of the lost figure strips historical structures to their minimum the same way Newman strips down his lines: Kierkegaard's lost figure of Jesus is itself abstracted to the point where it represents the injection of the universal into the particular. The difference is that abstract art begins with the human in order to approximate the divine, whereas Kierkegaard's Messiah begins from the divine and becomes associated with the human.

Initially, the black-on-black canvases are meant to mark the appearance of the "transcendental signified," the nature of the "Real" itself. Through various incarnations this act of abstraction (the removal of signifiers to arrive at the One) becomes empty and meaningless; it itself becomes a mere sign: the transcendental signified becomes the transcendental signifier. The black canvas becomes the sign of "nothingness" instead of the mark of the foray into the Real, and becomes merely a picture of what abstraction itself yields. In its extreme, emptying the image of figuration leads the blackness to become an attempt to picture God instead of the attempt to stretch representation to the point where God is figured by being nonfigured. The removal of figuration in abstract art leads to the blank, empty/full canvas that stands at one moment as the picture of the unrepresentable, and at the next as an empty abstraction of the idea of the unrepresentable that functions as a sign in its own way.

From one finite incarnation to another, from Malevich to Reinhardt, two possibilities of the meaning invested in abstraction emerge. From the first black canvases that point to the presence of the transcendental signified, the kingdom shifts from being present "beyond," to being either absent or present only in the human realm, in which case there is no "beyond" to represent and we arrive at the postmodern project of portraying the sign as sign only. Representation becomes presentation as there is no realm of form to be re-presented through art.[14] In Malevich's words, "It turned out that nothingness was God." Malevich's "creature turned creator" announces, "I shall build the kingdom of heaven on earth and not in heaven—therefore I am God . . . I am the beginning of everything, for in my consciousness worlds are created."[15]

Suddenly the status shifts to the empty abstraction functioning as a sign of the unrepresentable without approaching it, signaling that the removal of all figuration does not point to the One but to a false purity of form that is cold and lifeless, a far cry from the fullness and presence of the transcendental signified.

The other possibility that emerges from the rejection of the definitive presence of the kingdom "beyond" is the decision to accept the radically indeterminate status of the kingdom. With this, the project of abstraction is again reborn in the New York School, where representation is characterized as an allusion to the vast, indecipherable unknown whose presence or absence is optional, and abstraction begins anew. This, of course, is why I have looked at the abstract painters without making necessary reference to God; why I have transposed the God function into act. As Newman writes: "Instead of making cathedrals out of Christ, man, or 'life,' we are making it out of ourselves, out of our own feelings. The image we produce is the self-evident one of revelation, real and concrete, that can be understood by anyone."[16]

As was partly explained in the opening pages, the project of the abstract expressionists is to catch a glimpse of that which is the condition of existence. Kierkegaard's process of "coming-into-being" covers the becoming all things on the model of the divine intervention between actuality and possibility. Newman, Reinhardt, and Malevich attempt to bear pictorial witness to the same question: that of the condition of existence, by attempting to represent the unrepresentable. Here I will briefly go over what it is about the act of the artist that leads me to draw a parallel between it and the act of God now redefined as finite act.

The vast empty/full paintings of Newman, Reinhardt, and Malevich are indicative of act in that they endeavor to produce emptiness, a finite act of creation confounded by its own reversal. This is significant because the act then asserts its own sense of totality in that the painting does not need to refer to any outside, antecedent conditions. Its stance is as totality itself. This is Lyotard's point when he says, "The inexpressible does not reside in an over there, in another work, or another time, but in this: *that something happens.*"[17]

LIMIT AND PARADOX

There are two senses of paradox I would like to examine here. In Kierkegaard the first paradox is that his writing revolves around the silent gesture to the inexpressible. His expression pivots on notions of limit. He constructs a process of writing that is fundamentally indirect because it needs to articulate what is inarticulable. For abstract art, this paradox is evident in Newman's *Onements*, a series that functions around Heideggerian notions of withdrawing and revealing, and the silent gesture of indirection that points away from the work. The second sense of paradox in Kierkegaard is that his philosophy, in order to discover the universal, must be manifest in the particular, that is, God functions via manifestation in the human realm. Similarly, the paradox of abstraction is its mandate to represent the unrepresentable, that is, to make manifest what is "beyond" human understanding. This paradox parallels Kierkegaard's divine disruption in that it stretches of the limit of representation to insert the inexpressible in the realm of the expressible.

First I would like to look at the paradox implicit in Kierkegaard's project of elucidating the schism between the human and the divine. In effect, Kierkegaard is asking us to imagine the unimaginable. By writing indirectly he inaugurates postmodern notions of writing on the underside, in the crevices of language.

My point here is that in doing so, faith is conveyed through unsayable, impossible channels in language, through paradox, and that the language-rupture this produces is precisely what places him in relation to abstract artists, as they are trying to do the same thing with representation. Newman paints in the wounded space of representability, which is where Kierkegaard writes and where the reader is drawn when he/she is asked to imagine the unimaginable. All of this takes place in the rupture of communication, where communication constantly and asystematically attacks and retreats—reveals and withdraws—in order to mark out a place it can function, where it can be heard.

The signification of abstraction reveals and withdraws, in a semi-Heideggerian framework[18] that serves to explore the nature of the creative act indirectly, by deferring its "presence." Like Kierkegaard pointing to God, Malevich's *Black Square* gestures to the unimaginable in order to illustrate the fluctuating presence/absence of the totality of the fullness of the creative act. Newman's paintings operate on the sense of concealment and withdrawal implicit in the finite operations of the act of existence: in order to reveal the universe the creative act must withdraw because it is in the space of withdrawal that difference is revealed. Therefore the fullness of being is always deferred, never present.

Newman explores this gesture in his *Onement* series, which constantly points away from one painting in the series to another, and again to another, as it is an infinite series of "Onements," the presence of whose actual One-ment must constantly withdraw. Reinhardt, Malevich, and Newman avert their gaze from the Real in order to illustrate it.

Kierkegaard's God is revealed only indirectly, by intervening in the human realm. God's "hand" is never seen in its true form (the universal) because it intervenes by becoming manifest in the particular. Just as Kierkegaard inserts divine intervention to disrupt the rational totalization of history, Newman, Malevich, and Reinhardt disrupt the possibility of a totalized system of representation. They stretch the system of the representable to the limit in order to approximate what is beyond. Under the rubric of finite creativity their paintings are irruptions of the inexpressible in the realm of expression.

Their paintings function to disrupt totalized representation by saying, in effect, "Don't look here," instead of saying, "Look at me, I am something you recognize," as do traditional systems of representation. They say, "I am nothing, everything. If you look here you will not see me," which is the paradox. They are painting paintings that beg not to be looked at, and which looked at, direct the viewer elsewhere.

Here we are talking about a vast elastic limit that separates the human from the divine, even finitely understood. Reinhardt spent his whole career hurling himself against the vast blackness of his canvases, attempting with each of them to paint the "last painting." What he failed to understand was that every painting stretches the dimensions of possibility a little differently in a way that makes it clear that there can be no end. One can only paint the last painting repeatedly, over and over again. Representation is not static because the relationship between the human and the divine itself is dynamic, constantly changing sites and positions so that there is no longer a stable place to occupy. This is how Kierkegaard inaugurates poststructuralism, and how the modernist project of abstraction prefigures postmodernism by revealing the untenability of a stable subject position for either the viewer or the painter, the writer or the reader.

Another point regarding the claim that abstract art and Kierkegaard share a common project is that they both assert a "leap" between the human and the divine that leads to the idea of limit. Kierkegaard obviously sees a clear distinction between the two realms, which can only be stepped over by God when God intervenes in the human realm. But what is left to human exploration is a limit that divides possible comprehension of the nature of the chasm separating the human from the divine. Kierkegaard is explicit about the ability of humans to understand this split. He says one cannot possibly imagine it unless one has successfully achieved the personal relationship with God that is only possible in the religious stage of existence. Only God can properly initiate this stage, and so the individual must wait to be called by God and then must pass into absurdity with God's guidance.

In Kierkegaard's framework the final stage before the achievement of faith is infinite resignation. This is the stage at which the individual "trembles" in the face of the divine. Faith itself is different from this infinite resignation in that it cannot be simplified to the complete renunciation of the finite but is instead characterized by a paradoxical unity of the finite and the infinite that results in the absurd.

Kierkegaard writes: "A purely human courage is required to renounce the whole of the temporal to gain the eternal . . . but a paradoxical and humble courage is required to grasp the whole of the temporal by virtue of the absurd, and this is the courage of faith. By faith Abraham did not renounce his claim upon Isaac, but by faith he got Isaac."[19]

Faith is the absurd act of simultaneously negating and affirming the created order. This means that to embrace faith ultimately is to grasp the enormity and significance of the infinite without renouncing the finite. In fact, grasping the infinite re-places the individual in the finite realm where he "dances" with the absurd, seeing the absurdity of the world in which he lives. He is accorded a further responsibility for himself and his selfhood by grasping the infinite. "In the face of an all-powerful master, the individual recognizes his finitude and becomes aware of his profound responsibility for himself . . . Freedom lies in freely appropriated bondage."[20]

This idea has two points of relevance here. The first is its echo in the paintings as they place the viewer in a sublime relation to themselves, inspiring terror at the unfamiliar representation. This terror, however, is necessarily false as it is only ever a simulacrum of the true enormity to which it alludes. The terror at this false void is absurdity. To face the simulacrum is to reaffirm the finite, because the false infinite is ultimately part of the finite realm. By confronting this "exalted" sphere, what Newman, Malevich, and Reinhardt require us to do is to reaffirm the human realm, to reaffirm the imaginable via the "unimaginable" limit.

Confrontation with the limit reaffirms both what is beyond and before it. The human sphere stands in stark relief to the divine, and in the end the human is all that is accessible. The more the divine is expressed, the more the human is emphasized. This is also true for Kierkegaard's individual.

Kierkegaard's God interrupts both aesthetic immediacy and universal moral law, and ultimately occupies the paradoxical position of complete "otherness," which by its very nature problematizes what can be said about it. By writing in the crevices of language, Kierkegaard reveals that this "other" is an unthinkable that must nevertheless be thought.[21] Kierkegaard writes in order to lead the reader to the limit of "thinkability," at which time the unthinkable "other" approaches indirectly. The author withdraws so that an other (author) may speak:[22] in this way the "other (impossibly) 'speaks' by not speaking."[23] The withdrawal of the unspeakable is the condition of the possibility of speaking. Every word carries along with it its own rupture, so that within this rupture all saying is unsaying because indirect communication speaks through the failure of language. This failure of language is God.

This limit, then, functions the same way whether one is talking about the border between language and silence, between sound and noise, or the human and the divine. It becomes apparent that this project is about the nature of the intersection between the human and the divine, and the indirection that must accompany its thinking. The indirect passage between the human and the divine that is articulated in Kierkegaard's writing functions to legitimate the finite realm the same way that the abstract expressionists articulate the unrepresentable through representation. The limit that falls between the human and the divine ultimately closes off expression, representation, and language and folds them back into the finite function around which they necessarily revolve. The creative act must constantly be repeated and refigured in the struggle to signify it because the process of history and representation is never complete.

In conclusion, Kierkegaard's analysis of time and history in relation to God elaborates an account of creativity that is finitized in modern art. This "finitization" has close affinities with the modern philosophical conception of the act of existence and with the modern philosophers who follow in Kierkegaard's footsteps.

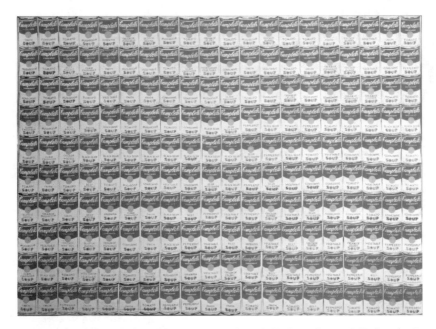

Figure 1. Andy Warhol (1928–1987). *200 Campbell's Soup Cans*, 1962. Synthetic polymer paint and silkscreen ink on canvas, 6' × 8' 4". ©2001 The Andy Warhol Foundation for the Visual Arts/Artists Rights Society (ARS), New York. Andy Warhol Museum, Pittsburgh, Penn., U.S.A.

Figure 2. Barnett Newman. *Vir Heroicus Sublimis*, 1950–51. Oil on canvas, 7′ 11 3/8″ × 17′ 9 1/4″ (242.2 × 513.6 cm). The Museum of Modern Art, New York. Gift of Mr. and Mrs. Ben Heller. Photograph ©2001 The Museum of Modern Art, New York/Barnett Newman Foundation/Artists Rights Society (ARS), New York.

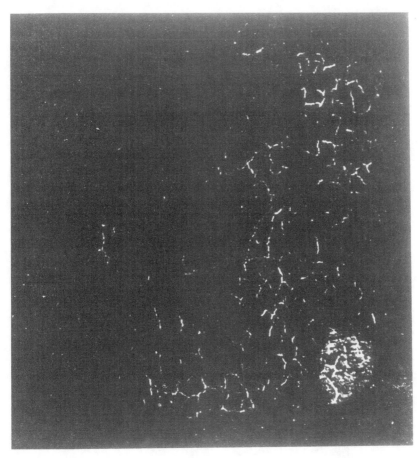

Figure 3. Kasimir Malevich. *Black Square*, 1915. ©2001 State Russian Museum.

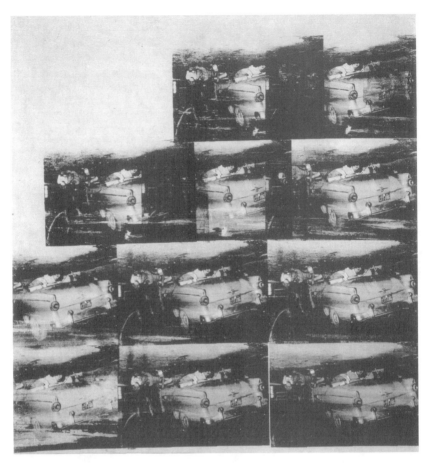

Figure 4. Andy Warhol (1928–1987). *Orange Car Crash*, 1963. ©2001 Artists Rights Society (ARS), New York. Galleria d'Arte Moderna, Turin, Italy.

Figure 5. Ad Reinhardt. *Abstract Painting*, 1960–66. ©2001 Estate of Ad Reinhardt/Artists Rights Society (ARS), New York.

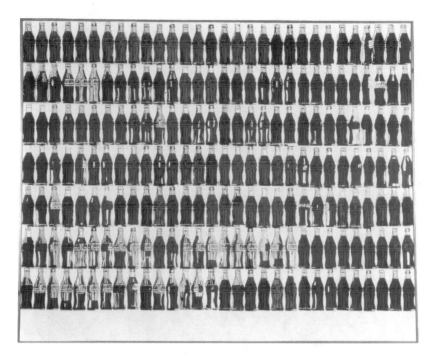

Figure 6. Andy Warhol (1928–1987). *210 Coca-Cola Bottles*, 1962. Synthetic polymer paint and silkscreen ink on canvas, 6′ 10 1/2″ × 8′ 9″. ©2001 The Andy Warhol Foundation for the Visual Arts/Artists Rights Society (ARS), New York.

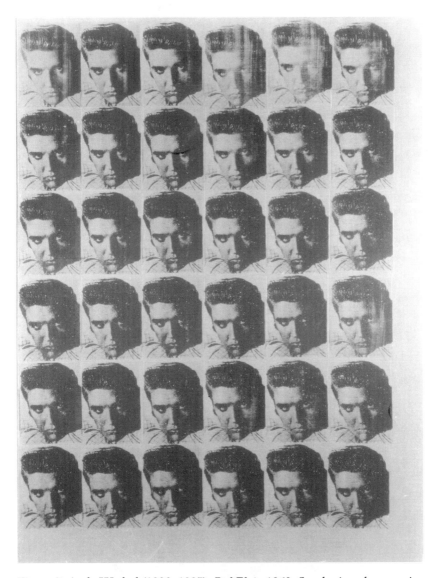

Figure 7. Andy Warhol (1928–1987). *Red Elvis*, 1962. Synthetic polymer paint and silkscreen ink on canvas, 69″ × 52″. ©2001 The Andy Warhol Foundation for the Visual Arts/Artists Rights Society (ARS), New York.

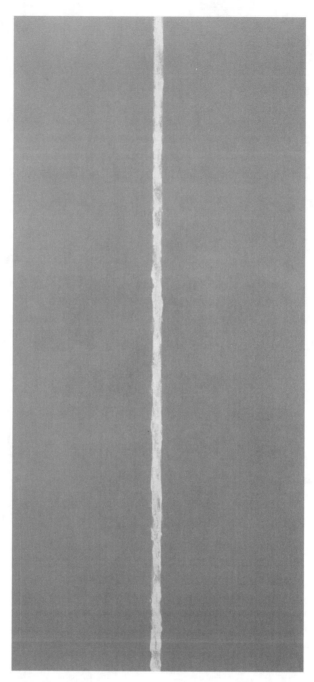

Figure 8. Barnett Newman. *Onement III*, 1949. Oil on canvas, 71 7/8″ × 33 1/2″ (182.5 × 84.9 cm). The Museum of Modern Art, New York. Gift of Mr. and Mrs. Joseph Slifka. Photograph ©2001 The Museum of Modern Art, New York/Barnett Newman Foundation/Artists Rights Society (ARS), New York.

Figure 9. Andy Warhol. *Orange Car Crash Fourteen Times*, 1963. Synthetic polymer paint and silkscreen on canvas, two panels, overall: 8′ 9 7/8″ × 13′ 8 1/8″ (268.9 × 416.9 cm). The Museum of Modern Art, New York. Gift of Philip Johnson. Photograph ©2001 The Museum of Modern Art, New York/Andy Warhol Foundation for the Visual Arts/Artists Rights Society (ARS), New York.

Figure 10. Ad Reinhardt (1913–1967). *Abstract Painting No. 5*, 1962. Tate Gallery, London, Great Britain. ©2001 Estate of Ad Reinhardt/Artists Rights Society (ARS), New York.

Chapter Three

Warhol and Kenosis

I<small>N THIS CHAPTER</small> I <small>WOULD LIKE</small> to compare Andy Warhol's art to Thomas J. J Altizer's radically immanent God in order to suggest that the notion of kenosis Altizer develops is a useful model for interpreting Warhol. I will also look at Heidegger's essay "The Origin of the Work of Art" in order to show that Heidegger's theory of presencing can be paralleled with Altizer's immanent God as a principle of kenotic metamorphosis. I will apply Altizer's theory of the radical immanence of God and Heidegger's theories of art to Warhol's work in order to show that the redemption of the image in the absence of God gestures to the transcendent. Using the framework offered by Altizer and Heidegger, I would like to offer four analyses of Warhol's art.

In the first two sections of this analysis I will look at presence and absence in Altizer. It is helpful to look at Altizer's theory of immanence because Warhol's art summons a "present absence" similar to Altizer's by presenting an image devoid of meaning. In the next section I will look at the principle of metamorphosis that emerges from Altizer's theology and the ways in which this principle applies to the process of emptying out meaning that functions in Warhol's transcendence. I will relate Altizer's process of metamorphosis, the process by which God is actualized in the immanent realm, to Heidegger's self-originating, self-sustaining truth that presences in the work of art, and show that both principles have the same implications for an examination of Warhol's absolutization of the image.

THE "PRESENT ABSENCE"

Thomas J. J. Altizer, in his book *The Gospel of Christian Atheism*, develops a radical theology that declares the death of God.[1] Altizer's rejection of

God signals the rejection of a transcendent God, but this is not to be mistaken for a total negation of the divine. Altizer takes a Nietzschean stance by holding that the totally "other" transcendent God locates meaning beyond the grasp of the human imagination, which leads to a negation of the importance of the world and ends in nihilism. To avoid nihilism, Altizer replaces the divine in a radically immanent realm in which "every vestige of transcendence disappears."[2] Without the transcendent, "all-knowing"' God, the imperfect human realm does not reflect the divine realm "beyond," and therefore the images and appearances in the immanent realm are images only of themselves. With Altizer's shift there is no longer anything "out there" tethering images to something beyond the immanent realm that gives them significance. As Mark C. Taylor puts it, "When the Kingdom of God is at hand, divine presence is totally realized here and now."[3]

Altizer's radical theology begins by attempting to reconstruct the Word of the Gospel within the immanent realm so as to place it in relation to the processes of history. He believes that the transcendent God, which remains outside the processes of history and human endeavor, becomes defunct if direct divine involvement in the human realm is impossible by definition. God as "other" is divorced from what Altizer sees as the primary function of the Word of God, i.e., the Incarnation and other divine interventions in the human realm. Altizer's God, once relocated in the immanent realm, empties itself out into the world and becomes all things. He calls this process of emptying out kenosis.

Altizer's move to the immanent at once brings the infinite to the finite and the finite to the infinite. Because God is no longer in the position of the "other" who tethers meaning in a ground "beyond" the human, the infinite descends into the finite realm and God becomes manifest in all processes of actualization. At the same time, things in the immanent realm attain the status of the divine as it is newly conceived. This connects image and appearance to God's processes of self-actualization, thereby redeeming appearances in themselves.

By "total presence" Altizer means that, with God's descent into the immanent, God's presence comes to be actualized through all processes and representations in the immanent. God's presence is thereby "total," extending into all aspects of the immanent, in contrast to what Altizer takes to be the earlier conception of God's presence as "other." When

God is transcendent "other," only occasional events bring God into contact with the immanent realm, as in the case of the Incarnation. This is what Altizer is seeking to amend with his theory of radical immanence. The implications of total presence will be developed further in the section on Altizer's dialectical metamorphosis.

METAMORPHOSIS

In Altizer's theory of immanence, instead of being a transcendent, inaccessible, unchanging entity, God becomes a principle of metamorphosis. As the infinite is finitized and the finite infinitized, God changes into a principle of kenotic metamorphosis. The essence of kenosis is that God empties itself out through the process of changing forms. The transcendent God becomes kenotic through the Incarnation, through which God changes into a human form, becoming "other-than-itself." In Altizer's estimation, the new immanent God is not a transcendent agent-creator but a God that is God's creative acts of self-unfolding. Altizer writes that the example of the Incarnation makes it necessary to construct God as a process of change whose nature is altered with and in the course of every event. In this scheme, God is present only in self-emptying and self-negation. Like Heideggerian "presencing," God reveals God only when God withdraws into another form.

It is Altizer's view that God is traditionally conceived of as an unchanging entity whose acts, if historically located, are fragmented demonstrations that are unrelated to God's eternal status as "other." He amends this notion with an appeal to the self-negation of God, which he locates as a necessary step in God's emptying itself into historically located forms. In Altizer's theory it is crucial that God remains God throughout the kenotic process. Taking the Incarnation as a starting point, Altizer argues that the nature of God's form undergoes a change from eternal and "other" into a process of metamorphosis when God empties itself into the form of Jesus. It is his view that this principle of change is a necessary development, for God cannot remain eternal and unchanging if God is inserting itself into the historical continuum in the form of Jesus. In radical theology this position underpins the shift toward total immanence. Altizer's point is that God ceases to exist in the primordial state of "otherness" when God becomes real in historical acts and events. This process marks the "making real" of God in actuality, that is, immanence. To maintain God's eternal "otherness" would be to refuse God's role in the historical continuum.

Altizer views the original Christian notion of God as being the process of making all things new, of "transforming the totality of history so that God may be all in all, therewith annulling all that distance separating the creature and the Creator, and obliterating every opposition between the sacred and the profane, or flesh and Spirit."[4] He wants to posit this process as absolutely real in that it actually makes flesh Spirit and Spirit flesh. As a principle of kenotic metamorphosis, the immanent God is constantly becoming other-than-God. God is now to be understood in terms of complete, nontranscendent, immanent activity.

HEIDEGGER AND ART

In Heidegger's essay "The Origin of the Work of Art" it is his view that the origin of the work of art "gives" art.[5] The work of art happens in and of itself, making space for itself through its being. The work of art lets the thing that is the subject matter arrive in the truth of its being. Heidegger holds that art lets the fullness of being presence through the work of art. The painting "speaks" the truth of the being of its subject matter, a truth that cannot be articulated any other way than through art. Thus Heidegger argues that art is an event, a dynamic activity that is "a becoming and a happening of truth." Because of the emphasis on the dynamic "presencing" of art it becomes evident that Heidegger is interested not only in the work as a revelation, but as creation. This leads me to draw a parallel between Heidegger's theory of presencing and Altizer's immanent God as a kenotic principle of metamorphosis.

For Altizer, God becomes the act of kenotic unfolding in the immanent realm. This amounts to the same thing as Heidegger's view that the work of art unfolds or presences the nature of its subject matter. Although Heidegger would deny that his system operates with any God, the God-function is served by the activity of presencing that echoes Altizer's self-unfolding God. By removing God from the transcendent realm, Altizer holds the view that the acts of God's self-unfolding happen in the immanent. By analyzing the work of art as dynamic presencing, Heidegger finitizes the notion of creation. Both Heidegger and Altizer deal with a groundless creativity that functions in the place of the traditional creator-God.

Like Altizer's kenotic God, Heidegger focuses on the unfolding of the fullness of meaning and truth in the work of art. For Altizer this unfolding is at work in all actualization within the immanent realm, whereas for Heidegger the unfolding takes place representatively in the work of art. Heidegger's world is wondrous and full of meaning in its unfolding—like Altizer's God, which endows the immanent with total presence, wonder, and meaning. Groundless creativity is at work in both cases: the immanent God kenotically empties itself into the world just as the work of art lets meaning presence.

SHOES

In "The Origin of the Work of Art" Heidegger provides an analysis of a Vincent Van Gogh painting depicting peasant shoes, probably one of two entitled "A Pair of Shoes," one dating from 1886 and the other from 1887. He writes: "Van Gogh's painting is the disclosure of what the equipment, the pair of peasant shoes, is in truth. This entity emerges into the unconcealedness of its being. . . . if there occurs in the work a disclosure of a particular being, disclosing what and how it is, then there is here an occurring, a happening of truth at work"[6]

Van Gogh's peasant shoes stand in stark contrast to Warhol's *Diamond Dust Shoes* (1980). In Heidegger's reading, Van Gogh's work reveals the self-validating givenness of the peasant artifact as it stands in its thingness. Heidegger argues that Van Gogh captures the givenness of the peasant shoes in the work of art by opening up the presencing of the shoes-in-themselves within the work.

Warhol, on the other hand, gives us *Diamond Dust Shoes*, a random scattering of women's shoes whose negative image is painted in bright acrylics. The single shoes float on a film negative without the other that would complete each pair. They are the picture of frivolity or fetish. In contrast to the earthy utility of the peasant shoes, whose leather Heidegger describes as intimating "the dampness and richness of the soil,"[7]

Warhol's shoes are surrounded and covered by the light-refracting, dancing glitter of diamonds. They are presented on a dark canvas literally streaked with diamond dust, a powder produced in the manufacture of industrial diamonds. The glittering diamond dust blanketing the canvas forefronts the surface of the image and acts as a screen between the viewer and the object that is meant to remind the viewer that there is no point of entry, no site of identification available. As is always the case in Warhol's work, the object stands alone, brought to the surface of the canvas, without the intent to draw the viewer into the picture.

Given Altizer's shift to immanence, Warhol's depiction of the object is blank, empty, signifying that its surface is its essence. Like Heidegger's citation of the peasant shoes that disclose the truth of the being of the shoes, Warhol's presentation of the shoes discloses that their being is vacuous and insignificant. Warhol's shoes "give" the truth that they are only surface. The true essence of the object revealed in the work of art in Heidegger's analysis is revealed only as it is absent from the object in Warhol's works of art. Van Gogh's peasant shoes "speak" the truth of their being by being painted. Warhol's shoes "speak" but are silent. They have nothing to say.

WARHOL

Warhol's *Campbell's Soup Can* (1964) is an image of the image of the soup can. I say "image of the image" because Warhol's soup can is not a still life in which soup caps are present, but a blank reproduction of the image of the can. The can is emptied of meaning, of context: it is presented blatantly as the empty image of a thing that has already been divorced from meaning in consumer culture. Warhol's image of the soup can gestures to the soup can, which in turn gestures to the fact that the soup can itself means nothing. In effect, Warhol says, "Here is an image," rather than, "Here is an image of something in the world to which I am referring through the image." Warhol refuses to ratify any connections between the image and the meaning of the image.

He gives us *210 Coke Bottles* (1962), *Twenty Jackies* (1964), fifty-four *Troy Donahues* (1962), and thirty-six Elvises in *Red Elvis* (1962). The replicability of the image is offered in Warhol's art rather than the image-in-itself. It is not the singularity of the celebrity or object that

Warhol is fascinated with, but its replicability and its status as an image of an image.

Just as Warhol's *Diamond Dust Shoes* "speak" and yet have nothing to say, Warhol's portraits are abstracted into the emptiness of perfection. His portraits make use of recycled media images of the celebrity that are brought into stark relief and then covered with brash blocks of color that only approximate the realistic colors of the face. As in the 1964 Marilyns, the bold blocks of yellow over her hair and blue over her eyes function to make the image recognizable—perhaps more recognizable than an absolutely realistic image of Marilyn—by abstracting Marilyn into an icon. It is clear in the Marilyns that Marilyn Monroe does not actually have yellow hair and eyes covered by blocks of bright turquoise, yet it is also clear after seeing the Marilyns that the blocks of color bring what is identifiable in Marilyn into stark relief. The icon-image of the celebrity replaces the celebrity; the image as image replaces the image of the thing. By perpetuating the perfected iconic image of the celebrity Warhol abstracts the celebrity into a state of nothingness that emphasizes the surface orientation of the Hollywood star-making machine.

As I have already mentioned, the images Warhol uses for his portraits are often repeated from film stills or publicity photos. In this way the image is "always already" repeated, a repetition of an image that in turn is a repetition of another. He also takes repetition one step further by repeating the repeated image within the portrait. The image appears over and over again in the series of frames within the frame of the canvas, and in addition to this, often appears in a series of canvases within a show or period of production. Warhol uses this technique for both his stars and his products. He adopts and perpetuates the commodified image of the star the same way he emphasizes the commodified product.

As is emphasized in his interviews, Warhol wanted to be a machine— a machine for recording that functions impersonally, objectively. Warhol recorded the objects that he reproduced without comment, objects as diverse as electric chairs, Coke bottles, and Andy Warhols. Warhol treats his own image as he would any image. In both his Coke bottles and his self-portraits he serializes and abstracts the object into pure image. His fascination with the object/product emerges from the desire to manufacture the same image over and over again to the point where it does not refer to anything.

FOUR ANALYSES OF WARHOL

The meaning of Warhol's image is a variable that constantly flips over on itself, from the meaningful to the meaningless, the full to the empty, always averting definition. His images are a play of/on signification; when pinned down, their meaning shifts elsewhere, always one step ahead of, or beyond, the game. Warhol's image refuses to settle in any one interpretation.

In this section I will present four interpretations of Warhol's art. The first view is that Warhol's art gives a nihilistic view of the world through his empty image, which conveys the impossibility of meaning in the world.

The second view is that Warhol's art presents a kenosis that is the same as Altizer's kenosis and the same as Heidegger's presencing of the work of art. According to this interpretation, Warhol's image unfolds kenotically, emptying itself out like the immanent God, and conveys a wonder in the emptiness of the image that is akin to Heidegger's wonder in the fullness of meaning.

The third view is that Warhol's art gives an inverse kenosis that gestures to the transcendent realm. In this interpretation the empty image points away from itself back to the transcendent. This view carries the implication that the focus on the immanent image is a way of representing the transcendent, which twists the project of abstract expressionism as it attempts to portray the fullness of the transcendent through the absence of figuration. In this analysis the emptiness of the immanent image portrayed in Warhol is actually a refiguration of abstract expressionism's project to figure the transcendent. It is an inversion of kenosis in that rather than inserting the divine into the immanent, the immanent image must gesture to the transcendent in an attempt to portray it.

The fourth view is that the transcendent, being beyond the limit of intelligibility, has the capacity to "give" meaninglessness in addition to meaning, and that therefore it doesn't matter how the work of art is interpreted because it points away from itself, telling us that the truth of art is not within art. This view holds that the transcendent does not necessarily offer meaning; it may in fact offer nonmeaning, meaninglessness, or it may withdraw meaning from the immanent. The fourth view, like the third, is a gesture to the transcendent with the difference that it is ultimately left open as to whether or not the image, emerging from the transcendent realm, has meaning. Rather than portraying the transcendent realm through the incessant repetition of the empty image as in the third thesis, this view asserts the possibility that the image gestures to the transcendent because the image portrays a positive meaninglessness that emerges from the transcendent. This view is an "inverted inversion" of kenosis; it proposes that the meaningless image may "give" from the transcendent in a kenotic unfolding, except that the unfolding is the unfolding of meaninglessness, rather than the meaning and fullness of Altizer's immanent God. It also differs in that it maintains the transcendent, rather than shifting God wholly into the immanent.

Nihilism

It is possible to conclude from the emptiness in Warhol that his images are ultimately nihilistic. I will not dwell on this possibility too much because it seems to be a common interpretation of Warhol's project. I mention it here to contrast with the fourth interpretation: that there is a way to have nothingness and nonmeaning without denying the possibility of meaning entirely.

In the event of the death of God without Altizer's immanence, the emptiness of the image amounts to nihilism. When God disappears there is only image, empty and insignificant. Warhol can be seen to draw attention to this meaninglessness by refusing significance and by emphasizing the arbitrary image divorced from a ground of meaning that redeems it. There can be no purpose or justification for the image or the world. In this analysis, Warhol shows us *210 Coke Bottles* in order to draw attention to them as serial products that differ only numerically. He chooses this object-product to emphasize that these objects are insignificant and that their infinite repeatability articulates the impossibility of meaning. Here Warhol's art is a critique of replication and of the notion that art can have meaning at all.

Warhol's series of Elvises and Troy Donahues, on a nihilistic reading, signifies the vacuous nature of the celebrity, which in turn signifies the vacuum of meaning of a world that attempts to endow celebrities with meaning. The soup can marks the critique of the revealed order of the commonplace, a gesture that criticizes the possibility of holding up the soup can as an icon. Warhol says, with his images, "so what?" In a world emptied of significance the image stands alone, unjustified, unredeemed.

By being absolute in their emptiness, Warhol's images reveal that something behind them has disappeared. Art becomes a sign of itself, in which "the thing becomes image and the image becomes the thing-in-itself."[8] The object in pop art does not point beyond itself because the image becomes the thing. Taylor writes, "since there is nothing beyond appearances, art embodies figures that are not only real but are the 'real itself.'"[9] What has disappeared, like Baudrillard's "original," is God, or transcendent meaning. In a nihilistic reading of Warhol the image is not redeemed by being the "thing-in-itself;" rather the empty absolutized image reveals that all there is is image.

In this section I have said that the emptiness in Warhol can be understood as a nihilistic position without wonder or meaning. In the next section I will consider the possibility that, in Warhol, emptiness is connected to wonder.

Kenosis

My second interpretation of Warhol's art is the view that it participates in a kenotic movement akin to Altizer's. As in Altizer's immanent emptying of God, Warhol's meaning is deferred from its transcendental site of God to the immanent realm where meaning is constantly in a state of metamorphosis, emptying itself into a new form the moment a form is actualized. Just as Altizer's God functions by the activity of unfolding in the immanent, Warhol's image unfolds through repetition. Whereas Altizer's God empties itself by unfolding into the immanent realm in a gesture that fills the immanent with meaning, Warhol's image becomes emptied in the progression of unfolding.

Warhol's image operates in the model of groundless creativity that is common to Altizer's metamorphosis and Heidegger's unfolding of presence. For Heidegger, presencing opens up the wonderment of the uniqueness and the fullness of meaning of the work. Rather than betraying a fullness, Warhol's image unfolds an emptiness of the image. I wish to suggest here that although what is being unfolded differs between Warhol and Altizer, and similarly between Warhol and Heidegger, the kenotic model is the same.

The application of kenotic activity is evident in Warhol's image as it is manifest in the incessant repetition of the image. Warhol's deification of the image becomes the visual manifestation of Altizer's radically progressive Incarnation. By producing the image in succession with other copies that show slight differences between the essentially repetitive frame, Warhol makes the kenotic movement manifest by emptying meaning through constant metamorphosis. Warhol transcends meaning by repeating it into nothingness, emptying out significance by incessant refiguration. Just as Altizer's framework presents the immanence of God as an expansion of God's realm, Warhol's kenosis expands the wonderment of the empty image.

The role of repetition in the presentation of the image points to kenosis because the image, when first presented, is endowed with meaning and significance, but through the process of being repeated in a series the image is emptied of meaning. In Warhol, meaning functions kenotically by unfolding itself in the succession of images.

In an Altizerian self-unfolding kenotic movement, Warhol empties his images of meaning through repetition. This is evident in his serial representations such as *210 Coke Bottles*, which repeat the image in order to frame the image *as image*. The emphasis on the serial nature of the product reveals that Warhol's fascination with the repeated, emptied image comes from the wonder of the possibility of such infinite repeatability. Warhol affirms each of the 210 bottles as something wondrous *because* they are repeatable.

Although Warhol's image presences in the Heideggerian sense, the consequence for the object in Heidegger's theory of presencing is one of total wonderment at the fullness of meaning. In contrast, Warhol's wonderment emerges from the absence of meaning in the image. Heidegger's world, in its giving, reveals the unique presencing of all things that emerge within it. For Heidegger, meaning emerges from presencing; for Warhol, meaning is removed. Warhol's object reveals the wonderment of the world by "giving" uniquely, like Heidegger's, but this wonderment is related to the absence of meaning. Warhol's wonderment in the world is at its empty seriality.

By removing meaning from the image Warhol reveals that it is the infinite repetition of the image, not the content of the image, that fascinates him. In contrast to Heidegger, whose world is wondrous because everything in it presences uniquely, the wonder of Warhol's world comes from the sameness of the consumer product. Framed this way, the relation between Warhol's emptiness and Heidegger's fullness of meaning is an inversion that displaces wonder to the singularly unwondrous: the empty and meaningless.

The givenness and presence of the authenticity of Van Gogh's peasant shoes does not differ from the artifice and fakery of surface in Warhol's *Diamond Dust Shoes* because both fit into the same frame of presencing the essence of the object. However, in Van Gogh's case, the presencing is of the being/meaning of the object; in Warhol's case, the presencing is of the being that is the nonbeing/meaninglessness of the object. Warhol's shoes focus on the empty essence of the surface-thing rather than the fullness of the presence of the meaning-thing. Warhol's image reveals that the wonder of the world is the absence of meaning. In this case the empty image "gives" the truth of its emptiness and reveals the emptiness of the world. This emptiness goes beyond an object's lack of meaning: this is an interest in emptiness itself.

Inverse Kenosis

My third approach to Warhol's art is that it inverts rather than echoes Altizer's conception of kenosis. In this analysis, the emptiness of Warhol's image does not operate kenotically like Altizer's immanent God but instead operates backward, from the immanent to the transcendent. Rather than echoing God's self-unfolding, the image almost seems to fold itself back up. The ambiguity of the image seems to draw the immanent back to the realm of the transcendent through the silent gesture away from itself in its enigma. What Warhol presents is referred elsewhere, to the "beyond" of the transcendent. In this analysis his soup can is not the soup can as an instantiation of the wonder of the self-unfolding immanent God, and it is not an apathetic reference to the meaningless object of the soup can: it is a reference to the limit of intelligibility, cloaked in the absence of meaning. It is a formulation of what is meaningless in the human realm because it is beyond the grasp of intelligibility, and what is meaningful in the transcendent realm but which remains inaccessible.

In this case, what appears to be emptiness in Warhol's image is in fact both a fullness and an emptiness. This emptiness approaches the transcendent realm from the immanent, reversing the movement from the transcendent to the immanent that is seen in Altizer. By approaching the transcendent from the immanent, the meaning that Warhol seems to reject is actually being re-formed, re-cast from the other side, shot from an angle that emphasizes the ambiguity of the possibility of meaning at all.

Warhol's ambiguity, in this reading, would be an ambiguity the same as that which must accompany thinking of the emptiness/fullness of the Neoplatonic One. It is the same ambiguity Derrida points to with *Différance*: the sameness that is difference; the double-edged, essentially elusive gesture away. Warhol's image refigures the condition of existence, the signified of the transcendental realm, by recognizing the limit of intelligibility that necessarily accompanies thinking about it. Warhol figures the limit that can be understood as the division between the divine and the human, the unrepresentable and the representable, the inexpressible and the expressible.

Rather than working with the idea that the absence of God untethers meaning in the immanent realm as in nihilism, Warhol embraces the unintelligibility of the limit by re-placing God, or what functions as God, beyond understanding. In this way, Altizer's radical immanence is the inverted model of what Warhol accomplishes.

This view does not seem to require the same inversion in an application of Heidegger to Warhol because Heidegger's view takes into account the withdrawal of meaning in concealment. In an effort to deal with Warhol's gesture back to the transcendent from the immanent, an inversion of Altizer's kenosis is necessary because Altizer's kenosis implies a unidirectional unfolding. In contrast, Heidegger's "giving" incorporates the concept of concealing. Because in Heidegger the work of art gestures to its origin, it is applicable to the way Warhol's image, in the inverted model, gestures to the transcendent.

Understood this way, Warhol's image gestures away from itself toward the transcendent, thereby shrouding the gesture in ambiguity. The gesture is double-edged: it at once implies that there is a meaning of the image that cannot be articulated without reference to the transcendent realm, and that the gesture to the transcendent is a dismissal of the significance of the mere immanent image. The duality of this gesture is the signal that signification, like meaning and representability, cannot be pinned down by definition, but must rather be deferred to the realm "beyond" the intelligible. Consequently, Warhol's image represents an apathetic gesture, the meaning of which must remain unarticulated.

Another possibility that emerges through the inversion of kenosis is that the gesture to the transcendent can be representationally traced in Warhol's images through repetition. The bold repetition of the serially immanent image can be seen to accomplish a figuration of the transcendental signified; that is, the portrayal of the transcendent realm itself. Abstract expressionism attempted to portray the transcendental signified by removing figuration, by opening up the vast inarticulability of the transcendent realm through blankness and the painted void.[10] Warhol's busy screen is meant to overwhelm, to flood the frame with repetititve images whose emptiness depicts the same inarticulable transcendent in noise rather than in silence.[11]

Normally presented as "Oneness," the transcendental signified is presented in Warhol's case and in Altizer's framework as the "manyness" of God. Here, Warhol figures the transcendental signified, by repeating the absolutized image into nothingness. When framed within an inverted Altizerian scheme of immanence, Warhol radically refigures the immanent image by figuring God, the "present absence" in his absolutized image, and by gesturing with an emptied image back to the transcendent. The figuration that is removed in abstract expressionism shows up in Warhol's work in the form of the absolutized image. While abstraction removes the image in order to figure the absolute emptiness of the transcendent, Warhol offers the empty image to signal that nothing is represented by the image. Warhol's image is the image of an image, the sign of a sign, which represses figuration by incessantly figuring what is insignificant. As in abstract expressionism, which represses figuration in order to figure the unfigurable, Warhol transcends what is shown and arrives at the transcendental signified as it stands in the immanent realm.

In this formulation, the repetition of the image of the Coke bottle signifies the radical reinsertion of immanent figuration into the representational estimation of the transcendent. The Coke bottles are shown because they are meaningless: they are shown over and over again because repetition empties the image even of its impact. Together these strategies create a smokescreen of images that stands between the viewer and the painted void. Being so bold and so commonplace, the images insist on full attention, but so much repetition stretches attention to the extreme. Rather than remaining attentive to one image, we are forced to consider them all, but because there are so many, we are quickly drawn into a different kind of painted void. This void is blatantly populated with immanent images whose collective insistence on attention draws attention beyond themselves, away to the transcendent.

Understood this way, the gesture to the transcendent implies that the transcendent is the realm of the meaningful. To hold that Warhol's empty image is empty because it attempts to figure the transcendent is to hold that the image figures the transcendent in order to gesture to meaning itself. In my final analysis I will show that there is an additional possibility that can be attributed to the gesture; that is, that the transcendent, being beyond the limits of intelligibility, is gestured to with the empty image in order to suggest that the transcendent may not be meaningful at all, that it in fact may have the capacity for meaninglessness.

Meaning and Meaninglessness

My fourth position is that Warhol's art raises the question of the possibility of meaning itself. Warhol's surface-image could reveal that it doesn't matter whether the image points to a fullness of being or an emptiness because meaning itself is ambiguous. Meaninglessness is no longer opposed to meaning; the two are the coiled surface of a mobius strip. In this view, Warhol's image refers to the transcendental realm with the gesture away, described above—only in this analysis, the gesture is complicated by the additional possibility that what is "beyond," in the transcendent realm, is not meaningful.

Here Warhol's gesture to the transcendent means that we cannot assume that whatever emerges from the transcendent will have meaning. Warhol's image leaves open the possibility that the transcendent— or the creative act in a finitized system—can "give" meaninglessness in addition to "giving" meaning. In this formulation Warhol is saying that the transcendent can "give" meaning but he also simultaneously maintains that it can "give" meaninglessness. Warhol is therefore not committed to the view that everything is meaningless, as is the case in the nihilistic reading, nor to the view that everything is meaningful, as is the case in both analyses of kenosis.

Warhol gestures to the transcendent with inverted kenosis; but here an ambiguity enters, which articulates something about the nature of the transcendent. Here is the possibility that because everything is united in the "beyond," meaninglessness as a positive (rather than a negative) value of meaning can emerge from transcendent potentiality to immanent actuality. This means that meaninglessness can be divine.

The gesture, therefore, is ambiguous in two ways. The first is that Warhol refuses to reveal what he means by the gesture, or by the image he gestures away from. If his gesture is read as a gesture to the transcendent—as was the case in the third analysis—it is still ambiguous what the nature of the transcendent is and why he is gesturing to it. But there is a second, more difficult mode of ambiguity that emerges here: the gesture is ambiguous because it positively asserts the total ambiguity of the divine or transcendent, rather than being ambiguous about what is at stake in the transcendent. It says, in effect, that God, or groundless creativity, or the creative act, has the potential to positively create, or "give" nothingness, meaninglessness, in addition to having the capacity to create or give meaning.

This sense of ambiguity opens up the possibility that the emptiness of Warhol's image is not an absence of meaning, or a nihilistic rejection of meaning, but is a meaninglessness that has the same status as meaning. It is the possibility that the empty image has a positive emptiness that in its emptiness is as significant as the positive fullness given by the peasant shoes.

Warhol is saying, then, that either fullness and emptiness are the same thing in the transcendent, or that whatever the case may be, the transcendent is totally inaccessible to the human imagination, so there can only be the ambiguous gesture. The transcendent, being beyond the limit of intelligibility, has the capacity to "give" meaninglessness in addition to meaning, and therefore, it doesn't matter *how* the work of art is interpreted because it points away from itself, telling us that the truth of art is not within art. The transcendent, being whole and wholly "other," may itself be ambiguous. The gesture to the transcendent is ultimately left open as to whether or not the image has meaning. This view is an inverted inversion of kenosis; it proposes that the meaningless image may "give" from the transcendent in a kenotic unfolding, except that the unfolding is the unfolding of meaninglessness rather than the meaning and fullness of Altizer's immanent God.

This "inverted inversion," however, differs from Altizer's radically immanent God in that it does not eradicate the transcendent when it implies a kenotic movement. Rather, I am suggesting a view of Warhol's art that has affinities with Heidegger's analysis of the artwork, which, as mentioned earlier, involves both concealing and unconcealing, with-drawal as well as "presencing." It is as if in the same way, Warhol's paint-ings posit the empty image as being "full" of meaninglessness rather than being empty of meaning. The consequences for this position are as follows.

First, if the image is "full" of meaninglessness rather than empty of meaning, and if this positive meaninglessness emerges from the tran-scendent, the empty image is potentially divine insofar as it manifests a meaninglessness that can mark the presence of God. This opens up the empty image for interpretation in three ways. First, it could mean that the image, whether empty or full, can be divine. This results in a return to the view initially explained in connection with Altizer and Heideg-ger.[12] Second, it can mean that the divinized image, whether empty or full, refers to the transcendent realm by gesturing to it or by picturing the emptiness, fullness, or fundamental unity of full and empty, which is the transcendent.[13] Third, it can mean that, given the transcendent's capacity for meaninglessness, whether the image is empty or full is not up to the work of art. As the first two options have been explored in the previous pages, I will undertake to examine the third.

Regardless of how the image is interpreted, the question of whether or not there is meaning is outside the realm of art. Art cannot do any-thing but hold something up and gesture to or away from it. Meaning depends on things other than art. Art cannot simply say, "Warhol's image is empty," because there is always something other than the art-work that must function in an interpretation of the artwork. This "some-thing other" can only be gestured to because it cannot be definitive. It could be the transcendent realm, the creator-God, groundless creativity, the social, the political, the ethical.

The surface quality of Warhol's paintings are at once unassailable in their integrity and flimsy in their inconsequence. Always without depth or perspective, the image is bold, unavoidable. Yet the solidity seems false, sometimes tenuous, as if the painting itself were a label that could be peeled off to reveal the groundless depth behind it. The soup can can be read in an infinite number of ways: as an exhortation to won-der in the singularity and uniqueness of the object (Heidegger); as a cri-tique of a society geared for endless replicability (nihilism); a signal to politicize and aestheticize the everyday (Benjamin); as just another image in the endlessly refracting house of mirrors that is signification (postmodernity); an attack on aesthetic elitism (the political); or as a mere celebration of surface. The interpretation is left wide open.

Warhol's ambiguity is unsettling: one way or the other, his image refuses to participate. Warhol's image calls meaning into question, but instead of being a pale echo of the postmodern crisis of meaning, the image seems to say that it simply doesn't matter whether the image is taken as a fullness of presence or an absence of meaning because it amounts to the same thing. All dualities, opposites, and interpretations are united in the single gesture to the transcendent. Whether Warhol's gesture to the transcendent ultimately emerges from the emptiness of the image or the fullness of the unique presencing of the object of the image, or whether emptiness and fullness are the same, the result is the same. Whether by kenosis or its inversion, Warhol's image gestures away from itself toward the transcendent realm, refiguring the unintelligible, inexpressible origin. By pointing to the transcendent, Warhol points to the emptiness and nothingness in addition to the fullness and meaning that may or may not be there.

Chapter Four

The Unrepresentable Event
in Heidegger and Heizer

IN THIS FINAL CHAPTER I WILL LOOK at the sculptures of American land artist Michael Heizer in the context of Martin Heidegger's essay "The Origin of the Work of Art"[1] and his book *On Time and Being*.[2] I would like to offer two theses regarding Heidegger's thought, which lead to a new understanding of Heizer's sculpture. The first is that Heizer's sculpture articulates Heideggerian notions of "earth" and "world." The second is that the spatial "abyss" at the center of Heizer's works is parallel to the "abyss" at the center of Heidegger's methodology. This abyss leads ultimately to the conclusion that Heidegger is interested in "figuring the unfigurable." I will look at the ways in which this idea emerges in relation to the work of art as it opens itself into world and earth and offer an analysis of Heizer's works as they open into a similar "openness."

First I will look at the basic thrust of Heidegger's argument in "The Origin of the Work of Art," specifically, that the work of art "lets truth originate." Next I will explain what is meant by world and earth in Heidegger, drawing in the terms in relation to the work of Heizer. Then I will look at the question of representation as it arises in connection with the opening up of world and earth (truth), and finally I will cast the unfigurable in terms of the incommunicable Event, showing that the Event is the unrepresentable, and that it is at work in Heizer's sculpture as much as in Heidegger's thought.

TRUTH IN HEIDEGGER

In "The Origin of the Work of Art," Heidegger claims that "art is the becoming and happening of truth."[3] The work of art lets truth presence.

In contrast to the Kantian view of art, which posits art in relation to states of mind (Kant's "disinterested pleasure") and that separates art from the "real" world, Heidegger's theory of the work of art asserts a strong connection between art and truth. Heidegger holds that the best way of understanding truth is through his notion of the thing. He dismisses traditional accounts of what the thing is, including the view that the thing is a subject around which properties are assembled, the view that the thing is a collection of sense perceptions, and most significantly, the view that the thing is a unity of matter and form. For Heidegger, all these conceptions miss the "thingness of the thing," which is the uniqueness and plenitude of the object.

In contrast to these traditional notions of the thing, Heidegger points to either of Van Gogh's 1886 and 1887 paintings of the peasant shoes, both titled "A Pair of Shoes." Van Gogh lets the peasant shoes "be" in his painting, giving us the opportunity to experience a "speaking and hearing" that occurs uniquely through the painting. The nature of Van Gogh's peasant shoes comes to light through the painting. The work of art lets the viewer know what the shoes are "in truth."

Because Heidegger is interested in the nature of the thing, he rejects the view that art is the expression of the creativity of the artist, or that the artist speaks through the work. Instead, it is the painting itself that speaks. Like Nietzsche, he maintains the view that art has a world-creating capacity: the death of God is also the death of the artist/author and the world is a "work of art that gives birth to itself." He posits a triadic relation in which the artist, the artwork, and the audience operate in a circle with no absolute beginning. None of the three are given a privileged position in the creation or interpretation of art itself.

The work of art is neither subjective nor objective for Heidegger. In its speaking, the work of art puts us in touch with a truth that we could not attain other than through art. The work of art, being independent from a creator, brings a self-sustaining and self-originating meaning into being. For him the work of art is ontological and ontogenetic, a revelation and creation of truth and of Being. Art reveals and creates truth. Truth emerges through the opening between earth and world.

EARTH AND WORLD IN
HEIDEGGER AND HEIZER

In traditional accounts of the work of art the thing has been interpreted in relation to the distinction between matter and form. Heidegger rejects this distinction because in his view it makes matter secondary to form. In contrast, Heidegger offers the view that matter comes into its own in the work of art in a way that is not recognized when it is conceived of as something secondary to form. In place of the form/matter distinction he offers his theory of earth and world. He calls the new conception of matter "earth." Earth requires a recognition that the material of the work of art has a nature of its own that is a significant part of the "thingness of the thing." The materiality of earth in the work of art is the irreducible, unique plenitude of the thing, which cannot be subsumed under the "form" that it takes as part of the work of art.

Similarly, "form" in Heidegger's conception becomes "world." As opposed to the uniqueness of the materiality of the work, world is the realm of meaning and intelligibility within the work. "To be a work means to set up a world."[4] The world of a work is not merely a structure imposed on materiality that causes it to "disappear" in the work, but rather, world causes the irreducible material of things to "come forth for the very first time and to come into the Open of the work's world."[5]

Rather than being a mere opposition, earth and world work in an essential tension with each other, a "striving."[6] The unity of the work is a result of the continual striving between earth and world, uniqueness and meaning, a battle that characterizes the work-being of the work. World operates in a tension with earth in the work because the work opens the world and the earth shelters and grounds the work. Together, earth and world maintain the work in its being. This tension introduces Heidegger's notion of "openness" because the work opens up, and holds open, the world it creates and the earth on which it stands. Openness can be characterized as a process of manifestation or revelation of the real nature of things. Hence truth emerges through this openness; it manifests itself through the work in the tension between uniqueness and meaning, earth and world.

Because the work of art sets up and opens into its own world, the work of art is not tied to notions of representational truth. Truth is created by the work in its own world. It is "through the work and only through the work" that what is portrayed in the work "arrives at its own appearance."[7]

In his example of the Greek temple, Heidegger's earth and world operate in a tension that lets the gods to whom the temple is consecrated become present through the tension. He writes: "This view remains open as long as the work is a work, as long as the god has not fled from it. It is the same with the sculpture of the god, votive offering of the victor in the athletic games. It is not a portrait whose purpose is to make it easier to realize how the god looks: rather, it is a work that lets the god himself be present and thus IS the god himself."[8] The temple, or the sculpture of the god, does not figure the god; it lets the god be present in the tension between materiality and meaning.

The American artist Michael Heizer (b. 1944) was a key figure in the Earthworks movement, which was active between 1966 and 1976. Along with Heizer, Walter de Maria, Nancy Holt, Carl Andre, Robert Morris, and Robert Smithson are considered to be Earthworks artists. Earthworks, also called Land Art, marked a reaction against the commodification of the work of art, as well as a rejection of the museum. Heizer's works marked a retreat of the work of art into the physical isolation of the desert, and developed according to a notion of "site-specific" work: art that "defines itself in its precise interaction with the particular place for which it was conceived."[9]

Heizer chose to work with the space in the Western deserts because there he found the kind of "peaceful, religious space artists have always tried to put in their work."[10] Reacting against what he interpreted as a surfeit of commodity-driven, strictly formal museum-based sculptures, Heizer chose to exhume vast tracts of land in the desert in order to work in terms of open space rather than with the closed, opaque masses of traditional monuments.

Before completing *Double Negative*, the sculpture most central to this analysis, Heizer completed *Nine Nevada Depressions*, a varying series of incisions in the desert, and three works in a series entitled *Displaced-Replaced Mass*, in which huge slabs of granite from the High Sierra were brought to Nevada and set in concrete-lined depressions in the ground. Heizer proposed an entirely new syntax for sculpture, one that was based on space itself rather than focusing on the delimitation of a form that occupies space. Rather than having a surface that encloses the internal volume of a form, Heizer's works are composed of space itself; they create a void that opens into the space surrounding the sculpture. Heizer arranges the vastness of space rather than composing a form that occupies space.

Heizer's *Double Negative* is a cleft in the earth that is interrupted, or held together, by the space of a natural valley. Heizer exhumed two sunken enclosures, each 50 feet deep, running a length of 1500 feet across a natural escarpment. The 50-foot cleft is closed on three sides, open at the top, and uniform in its width. When standing within the cleft on one side, the drop to the valley is invisible. When seen from above, the cleft is interrupted by the drop into the valley, seeming to be two different clefts even though from the earth it is only one. The piece is an experience of the vastness of the space of the desert, across both natural and man-made chasms. The work is aligned around the tension of the openness of the valley, in addition to the tension of the openness of the cleft as it crosses over the valley.

Heidegger's notions of earth and openness have obvious connections to the principles that operate in Heizer's sculpture. Heizer's works concern notions of space rather than mass. They mark a displacement of earth that remains within the earth it displaces. The sculpture cannot be separated from its materiality because the actual sculpture exists only in the tension between the material and the space opened up by its displacement. Heizer chooses to work with the desert land because of the uniqueness and plenitude of the open desert, which are crucial for the sculpture. This is the earth of Heizer's work.

The world of Heizer's work is less pronounced, though still fundamental. Heizer, unlike some land artists, does not impose a figure into the earth. His sculptures work mainly with negative spaces—cuts, hollows, incisions—whose shapes are dictated by the land into which they are inscribed. It is negative space in that it is carved into the ground rather than offering a positively delimited shape. Rather than the spirals of Robert Smithson or the large grass women of James Pierce, Heizer's works do not represent the presence of something new upon the ground. Heizer works with negative spaces: he removes material from the site in order to form the structure of his pieces rather than introducing something new. Before the sculpture, the site is worldless, like the world-less stone that nevertheless "belong[s] to the covert throng of a sur-rounding into which [it is] linked."[11] Heidegger says that "a world is never an object that stands before us and can be seen." Instead, the world works with the earth to "liberate the Open and to establish it [in the] structure [of the work]."[12]

On one hand Heizer summons the absence of the gods; on the other he mimics the Event of coming-into-being through the process-orientation of his works. His sculptures cannot be removed from their sites.[13] The Heizer pieces gain additional significance with relation to Heidegger's earth and world when it is noticed that they signify a reac-tion to the institution of the museum. Earthworks, as a movement, reacted against the notion that the work of art can be divorced from the space in which it comes to be. The works object to the transforma-tion of the work from "work-being" to "object-being" just as Heideg-ger does.

Heizer's sculptures are etched into the earth, literally and figura-tively sheltered by the earth into which they are carved. They open up in the tension between world and earth, their worlds coming into being as the inscription of meaning onto the previously vacant, worldless sites of desert. The world of Heizer's *Double Negative* is the imposition of a structure onto a previously unstructured (worldless) track of desert land. The world, in Heizer's case, is literally in a tension with the earth, because the structure of the sculpture has the form of an absence, a rift dug into the sheltering earth of the site.

Double Negative is not the imposition of a shape into a space, but the imposition of the earth on the work. The conflict in these pieces, between negative and positive space, is what binds them together as works.[14]

Heizer's pieces are carved into the desert, bringing out the open-ness of the open desert in their structural rifts. The use of negative spaces in these works, such as cuts and hollows, almost seem natural, as though they belong in the landscape. These works withdraw and presence in the worlds they set up. They happen through bringing the openness into the "Open," when the open is "sketched out," in ways that are not available in ordinary objects. They bring this openness out of nothing, if nothing here means a site that is not culturally inscribed with meaning beyond its meaning as "emptiness."

FIGURATION AND THE UNFIGURABLE
IN HEIDEGGER AND HEIZER

I would like to demonstrate that the Event in Heidegger corresponds to what I see as the unrepresentable in the sculptures of Michael Heizer. "The Origin of the Work of Art" deals with art, where art is understood as a generic term applicable to any happening or presencing of truth. In contrast, the general notion of the Event is only fully developed in *On Time and Being*. Because the Event operates in all events of presencing, opening, and giving, it is applicable to the event of the becoming and happening of truth in the work of art. For in *On Time and Being*, Heidegger endeavors to think Being itself, to "think Being without beings." The Event, as it is described in this work, is at the center of all events of being and becoming. In my opinion, Heidegger's Event, as developed in *On Time and Being*, includes an incommunicable element that is the same as that which is at work in "The Origin of the Work of Art" in the form of what I will call the "unrepresentable."

Connected to Heidegger's rejection of traditional notions of the thing and his emphasis on the "thingness of the thing," which I explained in the first section, is his rejection of propositional, representational, and conceptual thinking. In *On Time and Being*, this becomes Heidegger's rejection of the possibility of any kind of representation of the Event. He opposes propositional thinking to another sort of thinking, an incommunicable "listening" that allows us to "follow the movement of showing."[15] In "Summary of a Seminar," Heidegger attempts to "speak of something that cannot be mediated cognitively, not even in terms of questions, but must be experienced."[16] In this section I will show that this incommunicable element in Heidegger's thought corresponds to an unrepresentable element in Heizer's sculpture.

With regard to his rejection of propositional thinking, Heidegger's notion of truth is beyond "the agreement or conformity of knowledge with fact."[17] Instead, truth is unconcealedness. This unconcealedness refers to the relationship between beings and Being. In the Event, both beings and Being come to light.

Heidegger departs from propositional thinking in favor of "it gives." It is his view that we can apprehend "it gives" by "thinking the 'It' in the light of the kind of giving that belongs to it: giving as destiny, giving as an opening up which reaches out."[18] This thinking happens in the realm of the uncognizable. It marks the "awakening" to the Event that must be experienced, and that cannot be abstractly determined. The "it" that "gives" is incommunicable. It is not a transcendent ground or realm, nor does it have the agency of a creator-God. Heidegger disengages the "it" that "gives" from notions of causality and production as well as from notions of the origin. So what is left? The Event. The Event is the "it" that "gives" and that is incommunicable.

This incommunicable "it" emerges in his discussion of poetry, which for Heidegger cannot be understood in terms of propositional language. As opposed to the propositional structure, poetry represents the collapse of thought and language in the sense that poetry lets language presence without imposing the representational grid onto the world, which Heidegger attributes to propositional-conceptual thinking. It is my view that nonrepresentational art acts the same way against the economy of representation in that rather than offering a portrayal, it attempts to articulate what is inarticulable *as* inarticulable.

The opening that takes place in the tension between earth and world in the work of art is the revelation of the incommunicable. It is the Event of the happening of truth in the work of art. The work of art brings something into being that could not have come into being any other way.

For Heidegger, the opening of the work is significant for what emerges in the process of this opening. As we have seen, Heidegger maintains that this opening does not reach back into a transcendent realm from which "truth" emerges. Rather, truth is created by the opening of the work, by the "giving." The Event of opening of the work of art reveals the incommunicable, irreducible Event of opening and giving. The event does not have to be transcendent in order to be recognized as operating at the limit of Heidegger's thinking. The Event must remain unexplained.

For Heidegger there will always be "more." The world is untotalizable because there will always be more meanings, more creation. Because human subjectivity cannot see all things at once, there will always be something concealed when something is revealed. There is a tension between this concealing and revealing that betrays the idea that something must always remain hidden. That which is hidden is incommunicable, the unrepresentable. The process by which things are concealed and revealed is the Event, which itself is hidden in the sense that it cannot be explained rationally. There is always something operating within the process of concealing and revealing that, by its nature, is incommunicable, that cannot be mediated cognitively, and that cannot be proven.

In "The Origin of the Work of Art," Heidegger explains that representation in the work is not significant in the process of the creation of truth. It is not the shoes that are significant in Van Gogh's painting; it is the self-creating and self-sustaining meaning that is brought forth by Van Gogh's painting. Heidegger rejects representation because for him things are not re-presented; rather, the work uniquely brings the nature of things into light.

As part of his dismissal of propositional thinking, Heidegger also rejects correspondence theories of truth. Truth in the work of art happens through the self-creation of the work. The opening that the work accomplishes in the tension between earth and world is the opening of truth because what is brought into being in the work refers to the realm of Being in the event of giving. Again, Heidegger would not want to say that this "realm of Being" is transcendent, but that the work opens the passage to the condition of being, which is the unrepresentable Event.

One of the ways the Event is manifest is through the "opening" of the work of art. The work is the bridge into the world from the condition of being that is beyond intelligibility; it is a site through which the Event emerges. Heidegger rejects traditional aesthetic ties to representational truth because for him the representation within a painting is secondary to the world that is brought into being through the work of art. The world (and its tension with earth) is always the most important thing for Heidegger, regardless of the representational content of the work. Whether the work is representational, figuring a pair of shoes, or is nonrepresentational and nonfigural, like Heizer's, it opens a pathway to an understanding of the condition of being.

This is the purpose of the emphasis on world and earth in the "opening" up of the truth of the work of art. The truth that comes to light in a work of art is significant for creating a world that is unrelated to what is represented in that work. It is the wonder and uniqueness of the work and the world that opens into "openness" through the work that concerns Heidegger. What is brought into being through the work is beyond the representation within the work.

Heidegger would want to say that nonrepresentationality is not required in order for the nonfigural summoning of the god to take place in the work, because for him representation does not re-present: it manifests the Event, opening up the possibility for the gods to emerge. It is important to keep in mind that his writings on the temple are metaphorical; that it is not the actual gods or the creator-God that emerge in this space. In his finitized system, there is nothing that actually comes into being from an outside, transcendent realm. But the process of opening, and holding open, allows this god-presence, as absence or as Event, to come into being in the work of art.

Heidegger is not looking at the representation inscribed in the structure of the work, but at the being of the work itself. Similarly I would claim that in nonrepresentational art such as Heizer's, where there are no shoes, only a negative "opening up," the incommunicable can be seen to be figured in two ways.

The first way the nonrepresentational work can be seen to figure Heidegger's Event is representationally. It is not a paradox that nonrepresentational art can be read representationally if it is understood that the nonrepresentational artwork may be literally trying to figure what is unfigurable. For an application to Heidegger, the work would be attempting to figure the Event itself. Because the Event is incommunicable and unfigurable by definition, in order for the work to "figure" it, the work must gesture away from itself, toward whatever is "beyond," which in Heidegger's case is only the Event.[19] Additionally, representational art can be read as having the same effect,[20] as is the case for Heidegger's reading of Van Gogh's representational peasant shoes. It could be said that Heidegger's "opening" is "figured" in Heizer's work if we were to interpret Heizer's nonrepresentational sculpture as if it were representational in this way. Heizer could then be understood as literally making the "Open" manifest in his works. Within this interpretation, Heizer's desert rifts and fissures would be read as representations of the unrepresentable Event itself.

But the thing representationally portrayed in the work is not significant for Heidegger in the least: it is the being of the work rather than the content of the work that is fundamental for his thought. The actual representation in the work obscures the vision of the unrepresentable, gesturing away from the painting toward something else. For Heidegger it would not matter if the painting showed *das Ereignis*, or King Kong, or a bowl of fruit. Because, as we have seen, Heidegger is not interested in the representational aspect even of representational art such as Van Gogh's painting of the shoes, it seems that there is a much more significant conclusion to be drawn in reference to Heizer's nonrepresentational sculptures than the conclusion that Heizer's nonrepresentationality is actually representationality.

Heizer's art is nonrepresentational in that it does not refer to anything other than itself as a process or work. It stands "for" nothing; it "is" the carving of the earth on which it stands. In this way, the structure of Heizer's work literally "holds open the Open of the world."[21] In the nonrepresentationality of Heizer's sculptures, the rift that is the structure of the sculpture opens into earth and world, allowing the god to be present (or a "present absence") within it. Because Heizer's sculpture is focused around negation and absence in its structure—as it is a series of voids, cuts, and hollows in the desert landscape—openness, the absent creator-God, and the Event figure into the physical structure of the work. Like Heidegger's temple, which allows the gods to be present through its structure, Heizer's depressions in the earth let the event presence in the work. Heizer is interested in the opening up and presencing of the work in a way that is similar to Heidegger. I have explored this theme in more detail in the section on earth and world.

But more significant for a reading of the ways in which Heidegger's Event comes to be figured through Heizer's works is the idea that Heizer's unrepresentable is aligned with Heidegger's inarticulable Event. The Event can be seen to operate the same way in Heizer as it does for Heidegger in his writing. The Event is mimicked methodologically so that a greater understanding of what is meant by the Event can be gained when it is translated into the workings of Heizer's sculpture. Heizer's works can be seen to mimic the Event itself by doing the same thing with representation that Heidegger does with writing, that is, to demonstrate the Event through a subversion of the text itself. This is what I would like to propose is at work in Heizer's sculpture.

The methodological abyss, which is the very basis for the "giving" of the Event of the work of art, is evident in Heizer's works. What is interesting here is that the opening, the incommunicable element that Heizer brings into being, is the opening of Heidegger's Event. I will look at the nonrepresentational aspect of Heizer's sculpture in order to arrive at the conclusion that Heizer is figuring the unfigurable the same way that Heidegger is articulating the inarticulable.

In Heidegger's theory of the work of art it is never the portrayal that brings the being of the work to light and therefore it can be said that all art, representational or nonrepresentational, refers to the Event of the giving of the work of art. This is significant for an understanding of Heidegger because it is different from both traditional aesthetic theory and from the way Heidegger is normally read on the topic of the work of art. Rather than looking to the "depth" and "meaning" of the peasant shoes that Heidegger sees becoming manifest through Van Gogh's painting, this interpretation means that the shoes themselves are never what Heidegger is talking about, that instead, Heidegger is interested in an unfigurable "being" that comes to light through the work of art.

In this interpretation, Heizer is simply attempting, in a more clearcut way than any other artist, to articulate the Event of the work of art through the work itself. In short, he can be seen to be doing with art exactly what Heidegger is attempting to do with philosophy. In this framework, Heizer's sculpture throws light on Heidegger's theory in a way that illuminates the nature of that theory more clearly than do Heidegger's examples do.

Heidegger attempts to articulate that which is inarticulable, that is, the Event, in his writing on both the work of art and in *On Time and Being*. Heizer is attempting to figure that which is unfigurable, and must necessarily remain unfigurable, in a Heideggerian framework of the work of art. Heidegger points to the inarticulable through his own way of using language, whereas Heizer points to the same element through a different medium, that is, representationality and the element of impossibility within representationality.

Heizer, like Heidegger, wishes to desert the notion that the condition of being is a ground. Heizer's negation whittles away at the ground in which it stands. Heidegger says explicitly that the ground of being is "groundless." But the notion of groundlessness is not a simple absence for either of them. It is the translation of ground into an absence that fluctuates between absence and presence.

Heidegger describes the opening posited at the center of his system: "In the midst of beings as a whole an open place occurs. There is a clearing, a lighting. Thought of in reference to what is, to beings, this clearing is in a greater degree than are beings. This open center is therefore not surrounded by what is: rather, the lighting center itself encircles all that is, like the Nothing which we scarcely know."[22]

Heizer's focus on negation, when taken in this framework, leads to the conclusion that he is attempting to figure negation without negating it. The tension between negative and positive space nonetheless results in a negative opening, a depth carved into the earth that is formed by the displacement of material rather than re-placement of another material upon the existing, "presculpture" material. The absence that is formed by this displacement is literally a double negative because it is a negated negation, a negation that has become positive by its presence. But additionally—and this is what makes me think that Heizer wishes to avoid negating negation—the presence of the sculpture is also an absence— of preexisting material, of meaning, of figuration. In order to figure negation, Heizer must fail to figure negation because the figuration of negation negates negation. Heizer's negation fluctuates between being present and absent in the tension that it opens up between negative and positive space, between earth and world, between figuration and non-figuration. Heizer stretches the economy of representation to include its own impossibility, its own nonrepresentability. In this way, Heizer's position is much the same as Heidegger's, who wishes to articulate a philosophical stance that refuses to be articulable, and that must be conveyed through notions of the presencing and withdrawal of meaning and intelligibility. Heidegger's Event of becoming is an activity that conceals as it reveals: Heizer's *Double Negative* is a structure that keeps deferring its own meaning so that the work itself, as well as the viewer's position in front of it, must constantly fluctuate between absence and presence, meaning and unintelligibility.

Michael Heizer's work, when taken in conjunction with Heidegger's notions of the Event and the work of art, leads to notions of a fluctuating relation between presence and absence, figuration and nonfiguration, representability and unrepresentability. The incommunicable Event figures strongly in Heizer's work, making it unique among many non-representational artists, as his use of negative space attempts to avoid negating negation in his portrayal of it, thereby portraying the inherent duplicity of the concept rather than fixing negation as a simple absence. Heizer refuses to pin down the space he opens up, and can therefore be taken in relation to Heidegger's notion of the Event. The "Nothing" for Heidegger, and consequently for this reading of Heizer, is the condition of Being, the ground and possibility for meaning and Being itself. He is saying that you can show the "Nothing" or you can show something on the way to pointing at the "Nothing." Heizer does both, or either, depending on the degree to which this analysis is accepted with reference to his works.

Notes

Introduction

1. Thomas J. J. Altizer, *The Gospel of Christian Atheism* (London: Collins, 1967), 96.

2. Altizer, *Gospel of Christian Atheism*, 148.

3. Ibid., 150.

4. Ibid., 150.

5. Conversation with Dr. J. A. Bradley, Memorial University of Newfoundland, St. John's, January 1999.

6. Altizer, *Gospel of Christian Atheism*, 151.

7. Thomas J. J. Altizer, "Word and History," in *Radical Theology and the Death of God*, ed. Thomas J. J. Altizer and William Hamilton (New York: Bobbs-Merrill Company, 1966), 137.

8. Ibid., 84.

9. This is explored this in detail in relation to the unrepresentable in "Kierkegaard, History, and Modern Art."

Chapter One: *Repetition and Utopia in Warhol and the Marquis de Sade*

1. It is in this way that Warhol articulates the death drive in American culture. I will address this further in the second section dealing with the nature of the separate universe of the Factory.

2. Peter Wollen, "Raiding the Icebox," in *Andy Warhol: Film Factory*, ed. Michael O'Pray (London: British Film Institute, 1989), 21.

3. *Sleep*, 1963, 16mm, 16fps, 6 hr., silent. John Giorno is the sleeper.

4. Andy Warhol, *The Philosophy of Andy Warhol: From A to B and Back Again* (New York: Harcourt Brace Jovanovich, 1977), 23.

5. Wollen, "Raiding the Icebox," in *Andy Warhol: Film Factory*, 21.

6. *Poor Little Rich Girl*, 1965, 16mm, 70 min. Directorial assistance by Chuck Wein. With Edie Sedgewick.

7. Pierre Klossowski, *Sade My Neighbour*, trans. Alphonso Lingis (Chicago, Ill.: Northwestern University Press, 1991), 31.

8. I will further discuss the ways Warhol subverts the Hollywood system with reference to utopia.

9. Klossowski, *Sade My Neighbor*, 40.

10. Paul Arthur, "Flesh of Absence: Resighting the Warhol Catechism," in *Andy Warhol: Film Factory*, ed. Michael O'Pray (London: British Film Institute, 1989), 149.

11. Warhol projected his films at 16 frames per second rather than the traditional 24. This literally leaves the viewer in the dark for half the time that is spent in the theater. Jonas Mekas writes that it is this method that "with an unnoticeable, single switch from 24 to 16 mental or formal 'frames'—with one single conceptual switch . . . transposes the 'uncontrolled' realism into an aesthetic reality that is Warhol's and no one else's." (in "Notes after Reseeing the Movies of Andy Warhol," 1970.)

12. Wollen, "Raiding the Icebox," in *Andy Warhol: Film Factory*, 17.

13. As quoted in ibid., 17.

14. Ibid., 39.

15. Ibid., 20.

16. *Lonesome Cowboys*, 1967, 16mm, 110 min., color. With Taylor Mead. Viva, Louis Waldron, Eric Emerson, Joe Dallesandro, Julian Burroughs, Alan Midgette, Tom Hompertz, Frances Francine.

17. Mark Finch, "Rio Limpo: *Lonesome Cowboys* and Gay Cinema," in *Andy Warhol: Film Factory*, ed. Michael O'Pray (London: British Film Institute, 1989), 115.

18. Klossowski, *Sade My Neighbor*, 32.

19. Ibid., n6.

20. It is necessary to clarify the reasons for Sade's fixation on the act of sodomy. Klossowski locates the outrage in this act as it emerges from the biblical taboo. He writes: "This biblical term, consecrated by moral theology, covers an action that is not limited to homosexual practice. Homosexuality, which is not an intrinsic perversion, must be distinguished from sodomy, which is. . . . Sodomy is formulated by a specific gesture of countergenerality, the most significant in Sade's eyes—that which strikes precisely at the law of the propagation of the species and thus bears witness to the death of the species in the individual" (ibid., 24).

21. Ibid., 32.

22. Ibid., 40.

23. He does this by subverting the Hollywood film tradition. I will explain this in more detail in the second section.

24. Klossowski, *Sade My Neighbor*, 40.

25. Ibid., 42.

26. Marquis de Sade, *Juliette*, trans. Austryn Wainhouse (New York: Grove Press, 1968), 350–57.

27. Mikhail Bakhtin, *Problems of Dostoyevsky's Poetics*, trans. Caryl Emerson (Minneapolis, Minn.: Minneapolis University Press, 1984), 122.

28. Ibid., 24.

29. *The Chelsea Girls*, 1966, 16mm, 3 hr., 15 min., 2 screen, color and b/w. Hanoi Hannah reel scenario: Ronald Tavel. With Marie Meneken, Mary Woronov, Gerard Malanga, International Velvet, Ingrid Superstar, Angelina "Pepper" Davis, Ondine, Alberte Rene Ricard, Ronna, Ed Hood, Patrick Flemming, and Eric Emerson.

30. Annette Michelson, "Where Is Your Rupture?: Mass Culture and the Gesamtkunstwerk," *October* 30 (winter 1984): 60.

31. *Kitchen*, 1965, 16mm, 70 min. Scenario: Ronald Tavel. With Edie Sedgewick, Roger Trudeau, Donald Lyons, Elektrah, David MacCabe, and Rene Ricard.

32. Thierry de Duve, "Andy Warhol, or The Machine Perfected," trans. Rosalind Krauss, *October* 30 (winter 1984): 13.

33. Wollen, "Raiding the Icebox," 23.

34. *Empire*, 1964, 16mm, 16fps, 8 hr., silent. Codirector: John Palmer, cameraman: Jonas Mekas.

35. *The Thirteen Most Beautiful Women*, 1964, 16mm, 16fps, 40 min., silent. With Baby Jane Holtzer, Anne Buchanan, Sally Kirkland, Barbara Rose, Beverly Grant, Nancy Worthington Fish, Ivy Nicholson, Ethel Scull, Isabel Eberstat, Jane Wilson, Imu, Marisol, Lucinda Childs, and Olga Kulver.

Chapter Two: *Kierkegaard, History, and Modern Art*

1. Barnett Newman, "The Sublime Is Now," in *Theories of Modern Art: A Source Book by Artists and Critics*, ed. Herschel B. Chipp (Berkeley and Los Angeles: University of California Press, 1968), 553.

2. This is the Greek concept of *aphairesis*, which stands in contrast to *apophasis*. Mark C. Taylor writes "The penultimate aim of aphairesis is the essence of the entity under consideration; its ultimate aim is the essential One that underlies the many that compose the phenomenal world." In *Disfiguring: Art, Architecture, Religion* (Chicago: University of Chicago Press, 1992), 86.

3. Jean Francois Lyotard, "The Sublime and the Avant-Garde" in *The Lyotard Reader*, ed. Andrew Benjamin (Cambridge, Mass.: Basil Blackwell, 1989), 199.

4. See Henri Bergson's "duration" in *An Introduction to Metaphysics*, trans. T. E. Hulme (Indianapolis: Bobbs Merrill Library of Liberal Arts, 1955), and Martin Heidegger in *On Time and Being*, trans. Joan Stambaugh (New York: Harper and Row, 1972).

5. Taylor, *Disfiguring: Art, Architecture, Religion*, 83.

6. Søren Kierkegaard, *Philosophical Fragments*, trans. D. Swenson and H. V. Hong (Princeton: Princeton University Press, 1962), 107.

7. Julian Roberts writes, "This is, perhaps, a rendering of the traditional theological position that possibility corresponds to matter, the inescapable 'base' component of worldly existence." In *German Philosophy: An Introduction* (Atlantic Highlands, N. J.: Humanities Press International, 1990), 200.

8. "Everything which comes into existence proves precisely by coming into existence that it is not necessary." Kierkegaard, *Philosophical Fragments*, 91.

9. Ibid., 106.

10. Foucault picks up Kierkegaard's use of repetition in order to trace refigurations between different historical epochs, yet his Marxist sensibilities require him to hang on to the idea that even through different refigurations history is a process that can be deciphered by reason.

11. Alan Bowness, *Modern European Art* (London: Thames and Hudson, 1972), 135.

12. As Mark C. Taylor does, for example, in the "Iconoclasm" chapter of *Disfiguring: Art, Architecture, Religion*.

13. *Aphairesis*.

14. This tactical shift from one method of producing "nothingness" to another is a bridge to "Repetition and Utopia in Warhol and the Marquis de Sade." It seems to me that the notion of transcending meaning through the repetition of the act differs from this project primarily in relation to the different content initially ascribed to the act itself.

15. As quoted in Taylor, *Disfiguring: Art, Architecture, Religion*, 82.

16. Barnett Newman "The Sublime Is Now," in *Theories of Modern Art: A Source Book by Artists and Critics*, ed. Herschel B. Chipp (Berkeley and Los Angeles: University of California Press, 1968), 553.

17. Lyotard, "The Sublime and the Avant-Garde," in *The Lyotard Reader*, 199.

18. In Heidegger's analysis in *On Time and Being*, the notions of concealing and withdrawing are tied to finite time.

19. Søren Kierkegaard, *The Sickness unto Death*, trans. W. Lowrie (Princeton: Princeton University Press, 1970), as cited in Mark C. Taylor, *Deconstructing Theology* (New York: Crossroad Publishing Company and Scholars Press, 1982), 16.

20. Taylor, *Deconstructing Theology*, 17.

21. Kierkegaard writes: "My whole huge literary work had just one idea:

to wound from behind." As cited in Taylor, *Disfiguring: Art, Architecture, Religion*, 309.

22. This refers, of course, to Kierkegaard's complex pseudonymous authorship, which functions to upset the stable authorial "voice."

23. Taylor, *Disfiguring: Art, Architecture, Religion*, 314.

Chapter Three: *Warhol and Kenosis*

1. Thomas J. J. Altizer, *The Gospel of Christian Atheism* (London: Collins, St. James's Place, 1967).

2. Ibid., 82.

3. Taylor, *Disfiguring: Art, Architecture, Religion*, 155.

4. Altizer, *Gospel of Christian Atheism*, 82.

5. Martin Heidegger, "The Origin of the Work of Art," in *Poetry, Language, Thought*, trans. Albert Hofstadter (London: Harper and Row, 1971).

6. Heidegger, "Origin of the Work of Art," 36.

7. Ibid., 34.

8. Taylor, *Disfiguring: Art, Architecture, Religion*, 168.

9. Ibid., 152.

10. I have defended this thesis in Chapter Two "Kierkegaard, History, and Modern Art."

11. By asserting that Warhol and the abstract expressionists figure the transcendental signified, I am not trying to suggest that they are necessarily successful in portraying it. The point is that both figurations attempt to figure what is unfigurable, the transcendent.

12. Kenosis.

13. Inverse kenosis.

Chapter Four: *The Unrepresentable Event in Heidegger and Heizer*

1. Martin Heidegger, "The Origin of the Work of Art."

2. Martin Heidegger, *On Time and Being*, trans. Joan Stambaugh (New York: Harper and Row, 1972).

3. Heidegger, "Origin of the Work of Art," 71.

4. Heidegger, "Origin of the Work of Art," 44.

5. Ibid., 46.

6. Heidegger writes, "The world, in resting upon the earth, strives to surmount it. As self-opening it cannot endure anything closed. The earth,

however, as sheltering and concealing, tends always to draw the world into itself and keep it there." Ibid., 49.

7. Ibid., 35–36.

8. Ibid., 43.

9. Jonathan Fineberg, *Art since 1940: Strategies of Being* (Upper Saddle River, N. J.: Prentice Hall, 1995), 322.

10. John Beardsley, *Earthworks and Beyond: Contemporary Art in the Landscape* (New York: Abbeville Press, 1984), 13.

11. Heidegger, "Origin of the Work of Art," 45.

12. Ibid., 45.

13. "Where does the work belong? The work belongs, as work, uniquely within the realm that is opened up by itself," ibid., 41.

14. Like Heidegger's tension between earth and world, Heizer's conflict between negative and positive space "does not let the opponents break apart; it brings the opposition of measure and boundary into their common outline," ibid., 63.

15. Heidegger, *On Time and Being*, 2.

16. Ibid., 26.

17. Heidegger, "Origin of the Work," 51.

18. Heidegger, *On Time and Being*, 19.

19. This thesis is similar to the one explored in "Kierkegaard, History, and Modern Art," in this volume.

20. This is the thesis explored in "Warhol and Kenosis," in this volume.

21. Heidegger, "Origin of the Work of Art," 45.

22. Heidegger, "Origin of the Work of Art," 53.

References

Adrian, Henri. *Total Art: Environments, Happenings, and Performance*. New York: Praeger Publishers, 1974.

Altizer, Thomas J. J. *The Gospel of Christian Atheism*. London: Collins, 1967.

———. *History as Apocalypse*. Albany: State University of New York Press, 1985.

———. "Word and History." In *Radical Theology and the Death of God*, edited by Thomas J. J. Altizer and William Hamilton. New York: Bobbs-Merrill Company, 1966.

Artaud, Antonin. *Selected Writings*. Edited by Susan Sontag. Translated by Helen Weaver. Berkeley and Los Angeles: University of California Press, 1976.

Arthur, Paul. "Flesh of Absence: Resighting the Warhol Catechism." In *Andy Warhol: Film Factory*, edited by Michael O'Pray. London: British Film Institute, 1989.

Attali, Jacques. *Noise: The Political Economy of Music*. Minneapolis: University of Minnesota Press, 1985.

Bachelard, Gaston. *The Poetics of Space*. Translated by Maria Jolas. Boston: Beacon Press, 1994.

———. *The Psychoanalysis of Fire*. Translated by Alan C. M. Ross. London: Quartet Books, 1987.

Bakhtin, Mikhail. *Problems of Dostoyevsky's Poetics*. Translated by Caryl Emerson. Minneapolis, Minn.: Minneapolis University Press, 1984.

———. *Toward a Philosophy of the Act*. Edited by Vadim Liapunov and Michael Holquist. Translated by Vadim Liapunov. Austin, Tex.: University of Texas Press, 1993.

Barthes, Roland. *Camera Lucida: Reflections on Photography*. Translated by Richard Howard. New York: Hill and Wang, 1981.

———. *Roland Barthes*. Translated by Richard Howard. Berkeley and Los Angeles: University of California Press, 1977.

Bataille, Georges. *The Accursed Share: An Essay in General Economy*. Vol.1. Translated by Robert Hurley. New York: Zone Books, 1991.

———. *Blue of Noon*. Translated by Harry Mathews. New York: Urizen Books, 1978.

————. *L'Abbe C: A Novel.* Translated by Philip Facey. London: M. Boyars, 1982.

————. *Literature and Evil.* Translated by Alastair Hamilton. New York: Urizen Books, 1981.

————. *Story of the Eye.* Translated by Joachim Neugroschel. New York: Urizen Books, 1977.

————. *Theory of Religion.* Translated by Robert Hurley. New York: Zone Books, 1992.

————. "Georges Bataille: Writings on Laughter, Sacrifice, Nietzsche, Unknowing." Translated by Annette Michelson, with essays by Rosalind Krauss, Annette Michelson, and Allen S. Weiss. *October* 36 (spring 1986).

Baudrillard, Jean. *Forget Foucault.* Foreign Agent Series. New York: Semiotext(e), 1987.

————. *Simulations.* Translated by P. Foss, M. Patton, and P. Beitchman. New York: Semiotext(e), 1983.

————. *The Transparency of Evil: Essays on Extreme Phenomena.* Translated by James Benedict. London: Verso, 1993.

Beardsley, John. *Earthworks and Beyond: Contemporary Art in the Landscape.* New York: Abbeville Press, 1984.

Benjamin, Walter. "The Work of Art in the Age of Mechanical Reproduction." In *Illuminations,* translated by H. Zohn. New York: Schocken Books, 1969.

Benvenuto, Bice, and Roger Kennedy. *The Works of Jacques Lacan: An Introduction.* New York: St. Martin's Press, 1986.

Berger, John. *Ways of Seeing.* London: British Broadcasting Corporation and Penguin Books, 1972.

Berger, Peter L. *The Heretical Imperative: Contemporary Possibilities of Religious Affirmation.* New York: Anchor Press, 1979.

Bergson, Henri. *Creative Evolution.* Translated by Arthur Mitchell. 1911. Reprint, Lanham, Md.: University Press of America, 1983.

————. *An Introduction to Metaphysics.* Translated by T. E. Hulme. Indianapolis: Bobbs Merrill Educational Publishing, 1955.

————. *Time and Free Will: An Essay on the Immediate Data of Consciousness.* New York: Harper and Row, 1960.

————. *The Two Sources of Morality and Religion.* Translated by R. Ashley Audra and Cloudesley Brereton. Notre Dame, Ind.: University of Notre Dame Press, 1977.

Berry, Phillipa, and Andrew Wernick, eds. *Shadow of Spirit: Postmodernism and Religion.* London: Routledge, 1992.

Bigelow, Pat. *Kierkegaard and the Problem of Writing.* Tallahassee, Fla.: Florida State University Press, 1987.

Blanchot, Maurice. *The Infinite Conversation.* Translated by Susan Hanson. Minneapolis: University of Minnesota Press, 1993.

———. *The Siren's Song: Selected Essays of Maurice Blanchot.* Edited by Gabriel Josipovici. Translated by Sacha Rabinovitch. Bloomington, Ind.: Indiana University Press, 1982.

———. *The Writing of the Disaster.* Translated by Ann Smock. Lincoln, Nebr.: University of Nebraska Press, 1986.

Bogue, Ronald. *Deleuze and Guattari.* New York: Routledge, 1989.

Bowness, Alan. *Modern European Art.* London: Thames and Hudson, 1972.

Bradley, J. A. "Act, Event, Series: Six Theses on Speculative Metaphysics." Paper presented at the Masters of Philosophy in in Humanities Colloquium, Memorial University of Newfoundland, St. John's, winter 1994.

Buchloh, Benjamin H. D. "Figures of Authority, Ciphers of Regression: Notes on the Return of Representation in European Painting." *October* 16 (spring 1981).

Burger, Peter. *Theory of the Avant-Garde.* Translated by M. Shaw. Minneapolis: University of Minnesota Press, 1984.

Butler, Judith. *Gender Trouble: Feminism and the Subversion of Identity.* New York: Routledge, 1990.

Carmean, E. A. "American Art at Mid-Century: The Sandwiches of the Artist." *October* 16 (spring 1987).

Carter, Angela. *The Sadeian Woman and the Ideology of Pornography.* New York: Pantheon Books, 1978.

Celant, Germano. *Art Povera.* New York: Praeger Publishers, 1969.

Chipp, Herschel B. *Theories of Modern Art.* Berkeley and Los Angeles: University of California Press, 1974.

Collins, James. *The Mind of Kierkegaard.* Princeton: Princeton University Press, 1983.

Crone, Rainer. *Andy Warhol.* New York: Praeger Publishers, 1970.

Crosland, Margaret, ed. *The Passionate Philosopher: A Marquis de Sade Reader.* London: Minerva, 1991.

Crow, Thomas. "Hand-Made Photographs and Homeless Representation." *October* 62 (fall 1992).

Deleuze, Gilles. *Masochism: An Interpretation of Coldness and Cruelty.* Translated by Aude Willm. New York: G. Braziller, 1971.

Deleuze, Gilles, and Felix Guattari. *Difference and Repetition.* Translated by Paul Patton. New York: Columbia University Press, 1993.

Derrida, Jacques. *Dissemination.* Translated by Barbara Johnson. Chicago: University of Chicago Press, 1981.

————. *Writing and Difference.* Translated by Alan Bass. Chicago: University of Chicago Press, 1978.

Dery, Mark. "Signposts on the Road to Nowhere: Laurie Anderson's Crisis of Meaning." *South Atlantic Quarterly* 90, no. 4 (fall 1991).

Doane, Mary Ann. "Woman's Stake: Filming the Female Body." *October* 17 (summer 1981).

Dolar, Mladen. "'I Shall Be with You on Your Wedding-Night': Lacan and the Uncanny." *October* 58 (fall 1991).

De Duve, Thierry. "Andy Warhol, or The Machine Perfected." Translated by Rosalind Krauss. *October* 30 (winter 1984).

Fenves, Peter. *"Chatter": Language and History in Kierkegaard.* Stanford, Calif.: Stanford University Press, 1993.

Fineberg, Jonathan. *Art since 1940: Strategies of Being.* Upper Saddle River, N. J. : Prentice Hall, 1995.

Fineman, Joel. "The Structure of Allegorical Desire." *October* 12 (spring 1980).

Foster, Hal. "Postmodernism in Parallax." *October* 63 (winter 1993).

Foucault, Michel. *The Archaeology of Knowledge.* Translated by A. M. Sheridan Smith. London: Tavistock Publications, 1972.

————. *Discipline and Punish: The Birth of the Prison.* Translated by Alan Sheridan. New York: Vintage Books, 1979.

————. *The History of Sexuality: An Introduction.* Vol.1. Translated by Robert Hurley. New York: Vintage Books, 1978.

————. *The History of Sexuality: The Use of Pleasure.* Vol.2. Translated by Robert Hurley. New York: Vintage Books, 1985.

————. *Language, Counter-Memory, Practice.* Edited by Donald F. Bouchard. Translated by Donald F. Bouchard and Sherry Simon. Ithaca, N.Y.: Cornell University Press, 1977.

Gidal, Peter. *Andy Warhol: Films and Paintings.* London: Studio Vista, 1971.

————. *Materialist Film.* London: Routledge, 1989.

Girard, Rene. *Violence and the Sacred.* Translated by Patrick Gregory. Baltimore: Johns Hopkins University Press, 1977.

Grossberg, Lawrence, Cary Nelson, and Paul Treichler, eds. *Cultural Studies.* New York: Routledge, 1992.

Hansen, Alfred Earl. *A Primer of Happenings and Time/Space Art.* New York: Something Else Press, 1965.

Harris, Peter. "Aquinas and Heidegger on Being and Truth." Paper presented at the Philosophy Department Colloquium, Memorial University of Newfoundland, St. John's, winter 1994.

Heidegger, Martin. *On Time and Being.* Translated by Joan Stambaugh. New York: Harper and Row, 1972.

———. *Poetry, Language, Thought.* Translated by Albert Hofstadter. New York: Harper and Row, 1971.

Hollier, Denis. "Bataille's Tomb: A Halloween Story." *October* 33 (summer 1985).

———. "The Use-Value of the Impossible." *October* 60 (spring 1992).

Hughes, Robert. *The Shock of the New.* New York: Alfred A. Knopf, 1988.

Huyssen, Andreas. "Kiefer in Berlin." *October* 62 (fall 1992).

Isozaki, Arata. "Theme Park." *South Atlantic Quarterly* 92, no. 1 (winter 1993).

Jameson, Fredric. *Postmodernism, or The Cultural Logic of Late Capitalism.* Durham, N.C.: Duke University Press, 1991.

———. *Signatures of the Visible.* New York: Routledge, 1992.

Johnson, Ellen H., ed. *American Artists on Art: From 1940 to 1980.* New York: Harper and Row, 1982.

Kant, Immanuel. *The Critique of Judgement.* Translated by James C. Meredith. Oxford: Clarendon Press, 1952.

Kierkegaard, Søren. *Fear and Trembling/Repetition.* Edited and translated by H. V. Hong and E. H. Hong. Princeton: Princeton University Press, 1983.

———. *Philosophical Fragments.* Translated by D. Swenson and H. V. Hong. Princeton: Princeton University Press, 1962.

———. *The Sickness unto Death.* Translated by W. Lowrie. Princeton: Princeton University Press, 1970.

Klossowski, Pierre. *Sade My Neighbour.* Translated by Alphonso Lingis. Chicago: Ill. : Northwestern University Press, 1991.

Koch, Gertrud. "The Richter-Scale of Blur." *October* 62 (fall 1992).

Krauss, Rosalind. "Originality as Repetition: Introduction." *October* 37 (summer 1986).

Le Grice, Malcolm. *Abstract Film and Beyond.* Cambridge: MIT Press, 1977.

Leiris, Michel. "The Bullfight as Mirror." *October* 63 (winter 1993).

Leroi-Gourhan, Andre. "The Religion of the Caves: Magic or Metaphysics?" *October* 37 (summer 1986).

———. "The Hands of Gargas: Toward a General Study." *October* 37 (summer 1986).

Levine, Steven Z. "Manet's Series: Repetition, Obsession." *October* 37 (summer 1986).

Lippard, Lucy. *Pop Art.* New York: Praeger Publishers, 1968.

Lucie-Smith, Edward. *Art Now: From Abstract Expressionism to Superrealism.* New York: Morrow, 1977.

Lurie, David V., and Krzysztof Wodiczko. "Homeless Vehicle Project." *October* 47 (winter 1988).

Lyotard, Jean Francois. "The Sublime and the Avant-Garde." In *The Lyotard Reader.* Edited by Andrew Benjamin. Cambridge, U.K.: Basil Blackwell, 1989.

Marx, Karl. *Economic and Philosophic Manuscripts of 1884.* Edited by D. J. Struik. Translated by M. Mulligan. New York: International Publications, 1988.

Megill, Allan. *Prophets of Extremity: Nietzsche, Heidegger, Foucault, Derrida.* Berkeley and Los Angeles: University of California Press, 1985.

Michaud, Eric. "Van Gogh, or The Insufficiency of Sacrifice." *October* 49 (summer 1989).

Michelson, Annette. "About Snow." *October* 8 (spring 1979).

———. "On Reading Deren's Notebook." *October* 14 (fall 1980).

———. "'Where Is Your Rupture?': Mass Culture and the Gesamtkunstwerk." *October* 56 (spring 1991).

Michelson, Peter. *The Aesthetics of Pornography.* New York: Herder and Herder, 1971.

———. *Speaking the Unspeakable: A Poetics of Obscenity.* Albany: State University of New York Press, 1993.

Nairne, Sandy. *State of the Art: Ideas and Images in the 1980s.* London: Chatto and Windus, 1987.

Nesbit, Molly. "Ready-Made Originals: The Duchamp Model." *October* 37 (summer 1986).

Newman, Barnett. "The Sublime Is Now." In *Theories of Modern Art: A Source Book by Artists and Critics,* edited by Herschel B. Chipp. Berkeley and Los Angeles: University of California Press, 1968.

Nietzsche, Friedrich Wilhelm. *The Portable Nietzsche.* Selected and translated by Walter Kaufmann. New York: Viking, 1975.

Pattison, George, ed. *Kierkegaard on Art and Communication.* New York: St. Martin's Press, 1992.

Popper, Frank. *Art: Action and Participation.* New York: New York University Press, 1975.

Proust, Marcel. *Remembrance of Things Past.* Vol. 3. Translated by C. K. Scott Montcrieff and Terence Kilmartin. Harmondsworth, U. K.: Penguin Books, 1984.

Rainer, Yvonne. "Looking Myself in the Mouth." *October* 17 (summer 1981).

Ratcliff, Carter. *Andy Warhol.* New York: Abbeville Press, 1983.

Robbe-Grillet, Alain. *The Erasers.* Translated by Richard Howard. New York: Grove Press, 1964.

Roberts, Julian. *German Philosophy: An Introduction.* Atlantic Highlands, N.J.: Humanities Press International, 1990.

Rosenberg, Harold. *Art on the Edge: Creators and Situations.* New York: Macmillan, 1975.

Ross, Andrew. "The Rock n' Roll Ghost." *October* 50 (fall 1989).

De Sade, Marquis. *The Crimes of Love.* New York: Bantam Books, 1964.

———. *Juliette.* Translated by Austryn Wainhouse. New York: Grove Press, 1968.

———. *The 120 Days of Sodom and Other Writings.* Translated by Austryn Wainhouse and Richard Seaver. New York: Grove Weidenfeld, 1966.

Sartre, Jean-Paul. *The Words.* Translated by B. Frechtman. New York: Vintage Books, 1981.

De Saussure, Ferdinand. *Course in General Linguistics.* Translated by W. Baskin. New York: Philosophical Library, 1959.

Sekula, Allan. "The Body and the Archive." *October* 39 (winter 1986).

Seuphor, Michel. *Abstract Painting: Fifty Years of Accomplishment, from Kandinsky to the Present.* Translated by Haakon Chevalier. New York: Abrams, 1962.

Shumway, David R. "Rock and Roll as a Cultural Practice." *South Atlantic Quarterly* 90, no. 4 (fall 1991).

Sitney, P. Adams. "Cinematography and the Analytic Text: A Reading of Persona." *October* 38 (fall 1986).

Smith, Paul. *Discerning the Subject.* Minneapolis: University of Minnesota Press, 1988.

Solomon-Godeau, Abigail. "The Legs of the Countess." *October* 39 (winter 1986).

Taylor, Charles. *Sources of the Self.* Cambridge: Harvard University Press, 1989.

Taylor, Mark C. *Altarity.* Chicago: University of Chicago Press, 1987.

———. *Deconstructing Theology.* New York: Crossroad Publishing Company and Scholars' Press, 1992.

———. *Disfiguring: Art, Architecture, Religion.* Chicago: University of Chicago Press, 1992.

———. *Erring: A Postmodern A/theology.* Chicago: University of Chicago Press, 1984.

———. *Journeys to Selfhood: Hegel and Kierkegaard.* Berkeley and Los Angeles: University of California Press, 1980.

———. *Nots.* Chicago: University of Chicago Press, 1993.

———. *Tears.* Albany: State University of New York Press, 1990.

Ussher, Arland. *Journey through Dread: A Study of Kierkegaard, Heidegger and Sartre.* New York: Biblo and Tannen, 1968.

The V-Girls. "A Conversation with October." *October* 51 (winter 1989).

Vallier, Dora. *Abstract Art*. Translated by Jonathan Griffin. New York: Orion Press, 1970.

Warhol, Andy. *The Philosophy of Andy Warhol: From A to B and Back Again*. New York: Harcourt Brace Jovanovich, 1977.

———. *Chelsea Girls*. 16mm, 3 hr. 15 min.New York, 1966.

———. *Empire*. 16 mm, 16 fps, 8 hr. Silent. Codirected by John Palmer. New York, 1964.

———. *Kitchen*. 16mm, 70 min. New York, 1965.

———. *Lonesome Cowboys*. 16mm, 110 min. New York, 1967.

———. *Poor Little Rich Girl*. 16mm, 70 min. Directional assistance by Chuck Wein. New York, 1965.

———. *Sleep*. 16 mm, 16 fps, 6 hr. Silent. New York, 1963.

———. *The Thirteen Most Beautiful Women*. 16mm, 16 fps, 40 min. Silent. New York, 1964.

Weiland, J. Sperna. *New Ways in Theology*. Translated by N. D. Smith. Dublin: Gill and Macmillan, 1968.

Weiss, Allen S. "Framptons's Lemma, Zorn's Dilemma." *October* 32 (spring 1985).

———. *Iconology and Perversion*. Melbourne, Australia: Art and Text Publications, 1988.

———. "A New History of the Passions." *October* 49 (summer 1989).

Whitehead, Alfred North. *Adventures of Ideas*. Cambridge: Cambridge University Press, 1933.

Wodiczko, Krzysztof. "Public Projections." *October* 38 (fall 1986).

Wollen, Peter. "The Field of Language in Film." *October* 17 (summer 1981).

———. "Raiding the Icebox." In *Andy Warhol: Film Factory*, edited by Michael O'Pray. London: British Film Institute, 1989.

Woolf, Virginia. *A Room of One's Own*. New York: Harcourt Brace Jovanovich, 1991.

Zizek, Slavoj. "Grimaces of the Real, or When the Phallus Appears." *October* 58 (fall 1991).

Index